FIELD of GLORY
NAPOLEONIC

Written by Terry Shaw and Mike Horah

OSPREY PUBLISHING
SLITHERINE

First published in Great Britain in 2012 by Osprey Publishing Ltd.

Osprey Publishing
Midland House, West Way, Botley, Oxford, OX2 0PH, UK
44–02 23rd St, Suite 219, Long Island City, NY 11101, USA
E-mail: info@ospreypublishing.com

Osprey Publishing is part of the Osprey Group

Slitherine Software UK Ltd.
The White Cottage, 8 West Hill Avenue, Epsom, KT19 8LE, UK
E-mail: info@slitherine.co.uk

A CIP catalogue record for this book is available from the British Library

Print ISBN: 978 1 84908 926 5
PDF e-book ISBN: 978 1 84908 927 2

Cover concept and page layout by Myriam Bell Design, UK
Typeset in 1786 GLC Fournier Normal
Cover artwork by Peter Dennis
Photography supplied by Old Glory UK, Offensive Miniatures, Steve Barber Models & Front Rank Miniatures
Diagrams by Baueda.com

WWW.BAUEDA.COM

Project management by JD McNeil and Osprey Team
Technical management by Iain McNeil
Project co-ordinator: Paul Robinson

Originated by PDQ Media, Bungay, UK
Printed in China through World Print Ltd.

12 13 14 15 16 10 9 8 7 6 5 4 3 2 1

Osprey Publishing is supporting the Woodland Trust, the UK's leading woodland conservation charity, by funding the dedication of trees.

www.ospreypublishing.com
www.slitherine.com

CONTENTS

INTRODUCTION

Field of Glory Napoleonic has been designed in an approachable and easy to learn manner that allows players to concentrate on realistic deployments and battlefield tactics resonant of this classic era. We have tried to capture the atmosphere of battles ranging from the period of the 1st Coalition against the French revolutionary armies in 1792 and ending with the 7th coalition and the final defeat of Napoleon at Waterloo in 1815.

The Napoleonic Wars is a name normally given to the series of military campaigns that gripped most of Europe between 1799 and 1815. As the name implies, the central figure in this conflict was Napoleon Bonaparte, who became the ruler of France in November 1799.

Tabletop wargaming with miniatures is an engaging pastime and once hooked you will be a wargamer for life and will be able to join the growing fraternity of wargamers worldwide. For many this era has a classic feel to it with colourful uniforms and no less colourful characters. There is a wealth of literature available, including contemporary accounts and diaries. Modern historical scholarship is still busily at work extricating an immense wealth of detail from less than a quarter of a century of rich narrative and records. Figure manufacturers of all scales have not failed to rise to the challenge of the period, modelling with increasing accuracy and artistry many of the historical characters and variants of virtually all the armies. The 'what ifs?' of this period are no less stimulating.

This book is designed to both explain the game and be a reference guide when playing. To make the rules easier to follow we have added examples, detailed descriptions and explanations of unusual cases throughout.

Throughout the rules text in *italics* indicates that there is more information to be found in other sections. You will also find numerous pictures and diagrams that will assist your understanding.

Napoleon and his Marshals on the Field of Glory

What you need to play *Field of Glory Napoleonic*:

- An opponent: Games can be played with one player on each side, solo, or with multiple players on each side.
- A tabletop/board – the 'battlefield'.
- Two opposing armies of miniature figurines painted and mounted on bases of the same width. These figurines can be of any scale from 5mm to 28mm.
- Terrain for your battlefield, such as hills, rivers, marshes and so on. These are all commercially available and described in more detail later.
- Dice: Normal cubes numbered 1 to 6 (d6). Ideally, each player should have about 10 of one colour and maybe 5 each of two other colours.
- A means of measuring distances: a tape measure or a set of measuring sticks marked off in inches, millimetres or *Movement Units* (MU).

MEASUREMENTS

Measuring distances in *Field of Glory Napoleonic* is by ***Movement Units*** *(MU for short)*. One MU differs in size depending on the scale of figures used. It can be either metric or imperial as agreed by the players or decided by tournament organisers.

The MU is different for the various figure scales and whether or not the preferred measurement system is metric or imperial. One additional measurement is used at times in the rules. This is the 'base-width'.

The different measurement units are:

	Metric	Imperial	Base-width
20–28mm figures	**40mm**	1 1/2 inch	60mm
12–18mm figures	25mm	**1 inch**	40mm
5–10mm figures	**20mm**	3/4 inch	30mm
Preferred measurement units are highlighted in **bold**.			

Where measurements are used in the rules all 3 figure scales are usually given with the 20–28mm measurement written first and the 5–10mm one last. (For example: 60mm/40mm/30mm)

BASES

A ***base*** is a rectangle on which model figurines are mounted. The number and type of figurines gives a visual representation of the troops involved. A number of bases, as specified in our companion army list books, make a ***unit***. These are the playing pieces in *Field of Glory Napoleonic*. All the figurines used in *Field of Glory Napoleonic* are mounted on bases of the same width.

When using 20–28mm scale figures, a base needs to be 60mm wide. For 12–18mm figures a base is 40mm wide. For smaller figures a base needs to be 30mm wide, although some double width 60mm bases may be used for convenience. The depth of bases and the number of figures which can be mounted on each base are listed in the *Reference Section*.

Field of Glory Napoleonic features a range of different **troop types** which reflect the variety that existed in armies of the period. Bases of different troop types are represented in a number of ways, but the standard for Infantry is 8 figures to a base, 4 wide 2 deep and for Cavalry it is 3 wide 1 deep. Artillery is one gun model plus 3 or 4 gunners to a base. *Skirmishers* and *Irregular* light Cavalry have a reduced number of figures on a base. Some of the commercially available infantry figures may not easily fit onto the standard base, in which case the player may optionally reduce the number of infantry figures on a base to 6.

Groups of bases are used together in the game to form Units. These units are defined by four parameters: **Troop Type, Élan, Training** and **Weapons.** It is this mix of parameters that allows *Field of Glory Napoleonic* to accurately portray the variety of troop types which existed in the Napoleonic period.

Spanish Line Infantry

MARKERS

A few markers are required for ease of play. These are:

- **Cohesion markers:** 2 different ones – *Disordered* and *Wavering*, with possibly a third marker – *Broken*. A further temporary marker may be used – Halted
- **Aide-de-camp (ADC) markers:** A number of command markers may be needed to represent *Command Points* to be distributed by the Divisional and Corp Commanders.

Cohesion markers

TROOP TYPES

Troop types are divided into 3 basic categories and then several sub-categories, according to how they moved and fought on the battlefield. Different troop types are based in different ways.

The three main categories are Infantry, Cavalry and Artillery, which are sub-divided as follows (see the *Reference Section* for further information).

INFANTRY

These can be: *Line* or *Light*. They may also be referred to as *Skirmishers* when operating in that formation. Line infantry are also further subdivided into *Reformed* and *non-reformed* based upon their nation's use of *l'ordre profond* (attack column) or *l'ordre mince* (line). Reformed regiments are mostly assumed to have introduced light infantry companies into their battalion formations and to have stopped using the line as their normal formation for manoeuvre during a battle.

Croatian Infantry advance

CAVALRY

These can be either *Heavy* or *Light*. Some of the heavier troop types may also be defined as *Shock*. Light cavalry in a single line of bases (Extended Line) move and may evade from charges as if Skirmishers. *Irregular* light cavalry in any formation are as considered to be *Skirmishers* for both movement and combat.

ARTILLERY

These can be either *Field* or *Horse* and will also be defined as *Medium* or *Heavy*. *Light artillery* also existed but these are included only as part of the various artillery attachments available, and so are not represented separately. Some nations may be allowed to use specialised Artillery such as *Rockets, Howitzers* and *Mortars*. Where there is evidence that these were deployed as separate units they are listed in our companion army list books.

ÉLAN

Some troops were better fighters because of their morale, training and/or weapon skills. *Field of Glory Napoleonic* has three categories of troop quality or Élan: *Superior*, *Average* and *Poor*. Some troops may additionally be accorded the status of *Guard*. Some armies contain a high proportion of *Superior* troops, whilst others mainly consisted of *Average* or even *Poor* quality troops. Generally, an army of poorer quality troops will be weaker than an army of *Superior* troops. To aid game balance, in *Field of Glory Napoleonic* poorer troops cost fewer points per base to compensate for this, and the poorer army can therefore be much larger (see the *Points System* section for more information on troop point values).

TRAINING

Field of Glory Napoleonic has four categories of training for the troops in an army:

Troops that are used to obeying orders and who have practiced moving together in formation are classified as *Drilled*. Troops that have spent a number of years doing so are classified as *Veterans*. Troops recently enlisted with little or no training are classified as *Conscripts* and troops with no formal training raised as ad-hoc units when required are classified as *Irregulars*.

WEAPONS

Troops are normally armed with muskets if Infantry, or sabres & carbines if Cavalry. However, there are other weapons that may be used by a limited number of troops in some nations. For example rifles and lances. Artillery was much more complex with a wide range of types of guns and howitzers of different sizes and power in use by the different nations, some of them using weapons captured from others. Inevitably it has been necessary to generalise and we have concentrated on the tactical and operational use made of them and of their effectiveness rather than their detailed ballistic characteristics.

COHESION LEVELS

All units begin the game in good order and we refer to this as *Steady*. As they suffer battle damage, their willingness and effectiveness in battle is reduced, resulting in changes to their **cohesion level**. These changes can occur gradually or suddenly and represent a combination of morale effects, casualties, battle fatigue and loss of formation.

There are four levels of **cohesion:**

- *Steady*: in good order and ready to fight (STY).
- *Disordered*: reduced in effectiveness, but still in the fight (DSR).
- *Wavering*: in a critical state, unable to fight effectively (WAV).
- *Broken*: no longer able to fight, fleeing, or about to flee (BRK).

IN SUMMARY

The four qualifiers: **Type, Élan, Training** and to a lesser extent **Weapons** are used together to describe a base of figurines. Although initially this may appear a little complicated, it will be picked up very quickly and allows the very wide variety of historical troops to be simulated. Our companion army list books describe the troop types in detail. A little knowledge of history will help with tactical decisions. For example, the *Superior Conscripts* of revolutionary France are much better when used to assault the enemy rather than used for a prolonged fire fight. The relevant strengths and weaknesses of each troop type will become easier to understand and master as you play the game.

GATHERING YOUR FORCES

The first thing that a player needs to play *Field of Glory Napoleonic* is an army. The rules are designed to be played with many different figure scales and with many different figure basing schemes (see the section *Using Figures Based for Other Rule Sets*).

There are many different methods of choosing an army to play with. The main ones are:

- A **historical refight:** A historical battle or scenario is chosen, with each player or team choosing which side to command. The historical composition of each army is converted to match the unit organisations and command structure used in these rules.
- **A 'what-if' battle or scenario:** This type of battle is designed and prepared based on historical what-ifs to create a battle that 'may' have occurred if different circumstances had occurred in history.
- **A campaign game encounter:** Campaign games are popular in wargaming clubs and societies. They allow players to make their own history, but can lead to battles between armies that never actually fought each other.
- **A head-to-head point based game:** This type of game is an entirely fictional encounter between 2 forces each selected using our points system described in the *Reference Section* of this book. As with campaign games, using this system allows for non-historical encounters between armies. However, it can also lead to battles where both sides are using the same army. Although it may look a bit odd, there is nothing wrong with the same nationality armies fighting one another. It can be explained as a fictional civil war or maybe French troops fighting each other for supplies on the retreat from Moscow or Royalists versus Bonapartists or units mistaking each other in the smoke of battle (e.g. Saxons attacked by French on the first evening of Wagram). There are many instances of commanders on the same side who hated one another (French, Russians, Austrians, etc.). Although they were more likely to duel each other, it is possible it may have escalated.

PLACING THE TERRAIN

The terrain is placed on the table, matching that of the original battlefield or location if fighting a historical battle or a what-if scenario. Alternatively our own Terrain layout rules may be used (see *Setting Up a Points Based Game*), which are designed to give a reasonable battlefield without unbalancing the battle too heavily in favour of either player.

The 95th Rifles advance across rough terrain

DEPLOYING YOUR ARMY

Each side now places his figures on the table using whatever deployment method he wishes. This may be pre-defined if fighting a historical battle or scenario, it could be defined by a neutral umpire, or our own deployment rules may be used (see *Setting Up a Points Based Game*).

ORGANISING YOUR ARMY

Each player's *command* will probably represent a mixed force of between 15 and 25 thousand men, which approximates to a 'corps' in the terms used by many armies in this era. The composition of this force will depend upon the type of game being played.

A historical refight will require players to research the armies involved and convert their research into the units and commands required by these rules. Instructions on how to do this are included in the section *Using These Rules for Historical Battles.* Players wishing to fight campaign games and one-off battles will be able to use our army list books to design and build their own armies, within the framework given in those books.

Each player's command will normally represent a single large corps of 2–3 divisions, but may also include an attached 4th division. In some cases the command may consist of 2 small corps. For ease of reference we will refer to a single player's command as a 'corps' throughout the rules. Each corps will have its own *Corps Commander* and models to mark its Line of Communications.

TABLE-TOP UNITS

In *Field of Glory Napoleonic* a single Infantry unit represents a demi-brigade, a regiment or a grouping of battalions based upon their battlefield role, which for ease of reference is referred to as a 'unit'. A Cavalry unit represents a regiment or grouping of squadrons and an Artillery unit a grouping of 2 or more batteries. For Infantry a unit would represent a force of between 1,200 and 3,000 men, for Cavalry this would be between 500 and 1,200 men, and for Artillery between 12 and 30 guns. The term 'unit' is used throughout the rules to refer to a single Tactical group of bases

FORMATIONS

In general, troops must be in one of the permitted formations with all bases in edge-to edge and corner-to-corner contact with each other, and with all bases facing in the same direction with the exception of Infantry in Square.

The permitted formations are as follows:

- **Tactical:** The standard battle formation used by both Infantry and Cavalry.
- **Extended Line:** sometimes referred to simply as *line.* Can be used by both Infantry and Cavalry.
- **Skirmish:** a formation used by light Infantry and light Cavalry only.
- **Square:** used by Infantry only.
- **March Column:** Used by both Infantry and Cavalry.
- **Supported:** also referred to as *Self-supported.* It is a type of Tactical formation available only to large units of Infantry or Cavalry.
- **Limbered:** used by Artillery only.
- **Unlimbered:** used by Artillery only.

See the *Reference Section/Troops* for details of these formations.

DIVISIONS

As a general rule each division will be designated as one of three types:

- **An Infantry division:** May not contain any Cavalry units, but may contain up to 1 Artillery unit. It must contain at least 3 Units.
- **A Cavalry division:** May not contain any Infantry, but may contain up to 1 unit of Horse Artillery. It must contain at least 2 Cavalry units.
- **A Mixed division:** Must contain at least 2 Infantry and one Cavalry units, but no more than 4 of either. It may also contain 1 Artillery unit. When using our accompanying army list books, mixed divisions may only be used as stated in the list for the army being used.

ATTACHMENTS

Players may choose to upgrade the effectiveness of their units by including up to 2 different attachments in each. The maximum number and type of attachments allowed to each army is defined in our army list books. If not using these lists the following restrictions should be used:

- The total number of attachments allocated to Infantry units may not be greater than the total number of Infantry units (large or small) in the army.
- The total number of attachments allocated to Cavalry units may not be greater than half the total number of Cavalry units (large or small) in the army (rounded up). If playing a historical game these restrictions may be ignored if actual orders of battle provide alternate formations.

There may also be exceptions to the above restrictions defined by our accompanying army list books. For example; a French Old Guard division may use 2 Artillery units in 1812.

COMMANDERS

A commander is an individual of high rank, responsible for influencing one or more units. Each army must have a *Corps Commander* and 2 to 4 subordinate or allied *Division Commanders.*

Commanders are represented by individual bases and can move independently or with a unit they have temporarily joined. With the exception of commanders, all bases must be part of a unit. A base representing a commander must be easily distinguishable from other bases in the army. All commanders have a ***command range,*** which is the distance within which they can influence units. They also have a number of ***Command Points*** which they use to manoeuvre troops under their command.

There are three levels of commander and those available to a particular army are set out in the companion army list books:

- ***Exceptional Commander:*** An excellent leader who is a brilliant army commander. He controls 3 *Command Points*. Napoleon, Davout and Wellington all fit into this category.
- ***Skilled Commander:*** A good commander, capable of commanding an army, or being a reliable

Wellington and his Generals at Waterloo

subordinate. He controls 2 *Command Points*. Archduke Charles, Eugene and Bagration probably fall into this category.

- ***Competent Commander*:** An average commander able to command a small part of the army or be a weak commander of a large army. He controls 1 command point. Most commanders fall into this category.

Additionally any commander may also have the following trait.

- ***Charismatic Commander*:** A commander who possesses great powers of influence and leadership over his troops. He adds a bonus to the *Cohesion Tests* of the troops he is leading. Any of the above 3 levels of commander may also be *charismatic*.

During the movement or recovery phases of his own turn a commander may move to and join any one infantry or cavalry unit of his own command, which is not already in combat. If a commander joins a unit he must be placed in edge contact with it. A commander is considered to be 'leading' any unit that his base edge is contacting. If it is contacting 2 or more units the player must state which unit he has joined. A commander leading a unit has his command range halved unless that unit is in close combat, in which case his command range is reduced to zero.

LINE OF COMMUNICATIONS

The 'Line of communications' (LOC) plays an important role in maintaining the morale and fighting cohesion of your army. An army must have an LOC which is identified by the positioning of a base 90mm/60mm/45mm square. It is placed in open terrain if possible with one of its side edges touching the player's rear edge and also on or touching a road leading off that edge (see *Deployment* rules). Preserving and protecting your 'line of communications' and threatening the enemy's were both important objectives during this era. The LOC base can be used to create a small diorama to further enhance the look and feel of the battle.

French Aide De Camp

WINNING THE GAME

A player wins the game if he defeats his opponent by inflicting a specified amount of damage. A game ends when one or both of the armies are defeated, or if players run out of time before this occurs. The victory may be upgraded or downgraded according to the victors ability to pursue his opponent – based upon the number of 'fresh' Cavalry units that both sides have remaining at the end of the battle.

PLAYING THE GAME

The game is designed to be played on a rectangular table with the following preferred size:

- 8ft x 5ft (2.4m x 1.5m) if using 20–28mm models or bases
- 6ft x 4ft (1.8m x 1.2m) if using 12–18mm models or bases
- 4ft x 3ft (1.2m x 0.9m) if using 5–10mm models or bases

Note that these table sizes are only 'preferred' sizes. Larger or smaller tables may be used with a change in army size to suit. For ease of reference table sizes will use the imperial measurements throughout these rules.

The game is played using a standard tape measure (either metric or imperial measurements can be chosen as long as both players/teams use the same). All dice used are standard 6-sided dice (d6). A dice is rolled to determine initiative, which is used to identify which player or team moves first. The player or team whose turn it is to move is defined as the 'active player'. The other player or team is defined as the 'inactive player'.

GAME SEQUENCE

Each player makes alternate moves, beginning with the player who has gained the initiative. The sequence for each move is as follows:

COMMAND POINT ALLOCATION PHASE

Corps Commanders allocate their *Command Points* to subordinate *Division Commanders*. This enables a player to concentrate his *Command Points* on the divisions that are performing the most important actions.

THE ASSAULT PHASE

This phase is where your troops attempt to get to grips with your opponent's troops. If the active player so chooses, any of his Infantry or Cavalry units that are within normal movement distance may attempt to move into contact with enemy unit(s). He must declare all unit(s) that will be attempting to close to contact the enemy and which enemy unit(s) each intends to contact, although actual hand-to-hand combat between Infantry formations was comparatively rare.

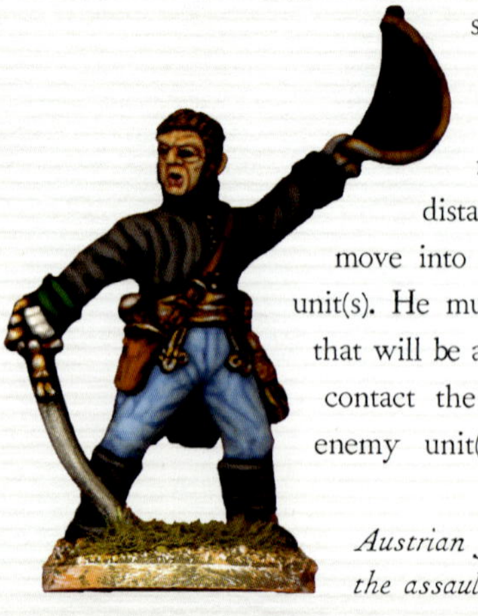

Austrian Jæger officer leads the assault

The enemy may choose to take one of 4 actions: stand, change formation, counter-charge or retire.

If the enemy chooses to stand, then, if Infantry or Artillery, he may fire defensively. If there is no fire, or if the fire is ineffective, then the assaulting unit moves into contact with the target enemy unit(s).

THE FIRING PHASE

Both sides get to fire their units in this phase.

The active player fires first with any or all of his units that are within range. Only close range fire is compulsory. Fire effects against each target are cumulative and results are calculated on each enemy unit in any order selected by the active player. Each target may only be fired at once per phase (even if fired upon by several different enemy units) and results are applied immediately.

The non-active player now fires any or all of his units that remain within firing range, even if his units have already fired once during the Assault Phase. Again each target may only be fired at once per phase with results applied immediately.

THE MOVEMENT PHASE

Only the active player moves his units in this phase.

The active player may move any or all of his units up to maximum of their movement allowance. Basic movement can always be performed, but some manoeuvres or formation changes may only be performed by expending a *Command Point* and after successfully passing a *Complex Move Test* (CMT). Other manoeuvres and formation changes may only be allowed to certain troop types. See the section entitled '*General Movement Rules*'.

Units cannot be moved into contact with enemy units during this phase.

THE COMBAT PHASE

Combat between enemy units in contact is resolved in this phase. See *Combat Mechanism*. At the end of each combat, one of the units will usually retire to reorganise or retire *Broken*. See *Outcome Moves*. In a few cases there may be a unit that will fight a second Combat Phase, but no unit will ever fight 3 times in one move.

THE RECOVERY PHASE

The active player tries to reverse the gradual disintegration of his army in this phase and may attempt to reorganise some of his units that have previously suffered some loss of cohesion. This includes rallying *Broken* troops and recovering abandoned guns. Note that units that have been heavily committed may never totally recover their full effectiveness.

DETAILED RULES

FULL ACTION SEQUENCE

The full sequence of events is as follows:

- **Command Point Allocation Phase:**
  - The active player allocates his *Command Points* from his *Corps Commanders* to his *Division Commanders.*
- **Assault Phase:**
  - The active player declares which Infantry or Cavalry units will attempt to assault the enemy this phase. He also declares any units of impetuous troops who are within reach of the enemy and who do not wish to assault.
  - The active player takes any *Complex Move Tests* associated with his declared actions expending 1 *Command Point* for each test taken.
  - The non-active player declares his reactions and takes tests for units where required before making the declared action.
  - Units which are making an intercept move or counter charging are then moved and intercepted units are moved into contact with interceptors. 1 *Command Point* is expended if the intercept move requires a CMT.
  - Artillery being assaulted may fire at medium range at the unit(s) assaulting them.
  - If an assaulting unit will be fired upon at close range the active player will move his units to a point 2MU from the enemy. The non-active player fires at these units at close range and applies results immediately.
  - The active player moves assaulting units to contact if allowed.
- **Firing Phase**
  - The active player fires his units where possible and applies the results immediately. The non-active player tests his units for any friends *Broken* by this fire and for units being burst through.
  - The non-active player fires his units and applies the results immediately. The active player tests his units for any friends that have *Broken* and for units being burst through.
- **Movement Phase.**
  - The active player moves any of his units and commanders within the restrictions laid down by the rules. He must move any and all units that are 'in command' first. He may then attempt to move units that are 'out of command'.
  - The active player removes one *Command Point* from one of his *Division Commanders* for every complex move attempt by a unit under his command. Once his *Command Points* are expended he may not attempt any further complex moves during this Movement Phase. (for more information on complex moves see *Detailed Rules/Complex Move Test*)
- **Combat Phase**
  - Combat occurs between friendly units and enemy units in contact with them.
  - Outcome moves are made.

Portuguese Cacadores

- Remove a base from Cavalry units that are *Spent* as a result of combat.
- Repeat these 3 steps once only for pursuing units if allowed.

- **Recovery Phase**
  - Assess victory conditions. The game ends if either side has been defeated.
  - The non-active player may move his commanders up to 4MU.
  - The active player may move his commanders up to 4MU.
  - Restore Artillery of both players to their original position within field fortifications if moved during firing.
  - The active player attempts to recover the cohesion levels of his units and recover abandoned guns.
  - The active player returns his *Command Point* markers (ADCs) to their respective commanders.

The individual elements of the action sequence listed above are described in detail in the following paragraphs:

COMMAND POINT ALLOCATION PHASE

In this section you will learn how to control and manage your units on the battlefield.

Command and control in the game is simulated by allowing *Corps* and *Division Commanders* and to some extent *Brigade Commanders* to influence the behaviour of their troops. We do this by making it easier for a unit to perform certain complicated moves if they are led by or within command range of a Commander. We also make it more likely that a unit will remain *Steady* or recover their morale state if within command range of their commander. Finally we gave a small bonus to units if a Commander leads them into combat.

General Poniatowski

Corps Commanders provide additional support to their *Division Commanders* that are within his command range in the form of bonus *Command Points*. He may allocate his *Command Points* to any *Division Commander* within his range during the *Command Point Allocation Phase.*

Division Commanders provide command for all units in their own division, but not for units in other divisions. Some armies can have one or more allied contingents. Allied commanders also provide line of command for all units in their own division, but are restricted in other ways.

The command ranges for *Corps Commanders* and *Division Commanders* are as follows:

	Corps Commander	Division Commander
Normal	20MU	8MU
Leading a unit	10MU	4MU
Leading a unit in combat	0MU	0MU

Brigade Commanders: Some armies are allowed to attach *Brigade Commanders* to their units. These commanders cannot leave their unit and act as a *Division Commander* only for that unit.

They therefore have an effective command range of 0MU. They are particularly useful in Cavalry brigades that may be required to operate separately on a flank. They have no *Command Points* of their own, nor may they receive additional points from their *Corps Commander*.

Allied Commanders behave exactly the same as any other *Division Commander* except that his *Corps Commander* must expend one extra *Command Point* when allocating additional *Command Points* to him. This means that a *Competent Commander* cannot allocate his one *Command Point* to an Allied commander.

COMMAND POINTS

All units can perform simple actions at any time without direction from their *Division Commander*. However, if any unit wishes to make a complex move or manoeuvre (see *Complex Move Test)* then that unit will require orders from his *Division Commander*. To simulate this we use ***Command Points (CP)***.

Command Points are supplied each turn by both *Corps Commanders* and *Division Commanders* as follows:

Skill level	Command points
3: *Exceptional*	3
2: *Skilled*	2
1: *Competent*	1

A commander may also be referred to as skill level 1, 2 or 3 instead of *Competent*, *Skilled* and *Exceptional*. This is often an easier way to remember the number of *Command Points* available to a commander.

A *Corps Commander* may allocate his command point(s) to his subordinate *Division Commanders*. In order to identify where he has allocated them, players are encouraged to use aide-de-camp markers (ADCs), 1 for each *Command Point*.

The skill level of a *Division Commander* affects the number of Complex Move Tests (CMTs) that the troops under his control may perform. For more information on the CMT see the section *The Complex Move Test* in the *Detailed Rules* section. The number of CMTs attempted each turn by the units of a division is limited by the number of unused *Command Points* controlled by their *Division Commander*. If the *Division Commander* has no unspent *Command Points* then no unit in that division may attempt a CMT. The exception to this is that any unit led by a commander of any type (Corps, Division or Brigade) may always take a CMT at any time. In effect this gives every commander a 'free' *Command Point* for the unit he is leading. A commander leading a unit in contact with the enemy cannot allocate *Command Points*, nor can the unit he is with attempt a CMT.

Rules for the use of *Command Points* are as follows:

- All *Command Points* are returned to their respective commanders at the end of a player's own Recovery Phase. Any markers/ADCs must be repositioned touching their respective commander bases. Unused *Command Points* are lost.
- A *Corps Commander* must expend a *Command Point* in order to move voluntarily. He must expend one *Command Point* each time he moves, excluding the 4MU allowed during either player's Recovery Phase. If a player has any plans to move the *Corps Commander*, he must retain a *Command Point* for this purpose. If forced to move during either player's turn he will automatically lose one of his unallocated *Command Points* unless he has none remaining in which case his forced movement is free.

French Aide De Camp

- The active player allocates *Command Points* from his *Corps Commander* to any of his *Division Commanders* at the start of his turn – during the *Command Point Allocation Phase.* He may allocate *Command Points* to his *Division Commanders* in any way he wishes, and may retain any for his own use. These *Command Points* are used to temporarily increase the command level of the *Division Commander* for that turn only.
- *Division Commanders* outside the command range of the *Corps Commander* require 1 additional point of allocation. That is, 2 points must be allocated from the *Corps Commander* to increase his points by 1, and 3 points to increase it by 2
- Allied commanders require 1 additional point of allocation. That is, 2 points must be allocated from the *Corps Commander* to increase an allied *Division Commander's* points by 1, and 3 points to increase it by 2.

Note that an allied *Division Commander* requires 3 points of allocation to increase his point by 1 if he is outside the command range of his *Corps Commander.*

- *Command Points* can only be allocated by *Division Commanders* to units in their own command. A *Corps Commander* cannot issue *Command Points* directly to units other than to move with a unit he is leading.
- One *Command Point* is expended for each CMT taken by units in a division. When a *Division Commander* has used all his available *Command Points* no further CMTs can be attempted that turn by the units of his division, unless they are led by a commander.
- If a *Divisional* or *Brigade Commander* is leading a unit, that unit can take a CMT without expending a *Command Point.* If a *Corps Commander* is leading the unit it may freely turn or reform whilst otherwise remaining stationary. Any other move by the *Corps Commander* will require the expending of a *Command Point.*
- *Command Points* may be required during the opponent's Assault Phase for Infantry and Cavalry units that wish to intercept, unless the intercepting unit is led by a *Division* or *Brigade Commander.*
- No *Command Points* can be allocated from the *Corps Commander* to the *Division Commander* of a reserve or flank marching command unless he is on the table during the Command Allocation Phase.

Saxon Infantryman

THE ASSAULT PHASE

At the start of each turn, the active player must decide whether or not to attempt to move into contact with the enemy (assault) with any of his units.

TROOPS ALLOWED TO ASSAULT

Only Infantry or Cavalry can make an assault move. To do so a unit must satisfy the following criteria:

- It must be able to see the target of the assault from the starting position.
- It must be able to make a normal advance move that will contact the target or the front of a defended obstacle.
- It is not Infantry in Extended Line and 'kinked'.
- It is not in March Column unless assaulting across a bridge, or its move is entirely along a road and it is assaulting into buildings.
- It cannot make a formation change.
- It must take a *Complex Move Test* (CMT), and its *Division Commander* must expend a *Command Point* (unless the unit is led by a commander of any type) in the following circumstances:
  - Declaring an assault which will pass through friends. These can only be *Skirmishers* or Artillery, or non-*Broken* Infantry who are part of the same division as the assaulting unit.
  - Declaring an assault with Cavalry against a target that is also being assaulted by Infantry.
  - Declaring an assault with mounted *Skirmishers* against the front of an enemy unit, unless all targets are *Skirmishers* or are *Wavering* or *Broken*.
  - Declaring an assault with a *Spent* or *Disordered* unit unless the assaulting unit is *Guard,* or is *shock cavalry*, or is an unspent *Impetuous* unit, or if the target is *Wavering* or *Broken.*
  - An *Impetuous* unit which is *Unspent* and either *Steady or Disordered* MUST take a CMT if they could contact an enemy unit but do NOT wish to assault it, even if such an assault would pass through friendly units they are not normally allowed to assault through. If they fail the test they must declare an assault on an enemy target in the following order:
    - The nearest enemy unit in reach and directly to their front.
    - The enemy unit that can be reached with the minimum amount of wheeling.
    - The nearest enemy.
    - If 2 targets are of equal priority the active player chooses which to target.

  A *Cohesion Test* must be taken by any friendly unit passed through by a unit which fails this CMT.
- A *Corps Commander* must expend one of his own command points if he is to lead a unit into an assault.
- Declaring an assault with a unit which is outside the command range of its *Division Commander* requires the expenditure of a *Command Point,* unless that unit is led by a *Corps* or *Brigade Commander.* If the assault would normally require a CMT then 2 *Command Points* must be expended.
- Assaults cannot be declared (or not declared by *Impetuous* units) if *Command Points* are required but the unit's *Division Commander* does not have enough remaining.

Assaults are not allowed in the following circumstances:

- *Wavering* and *Broken* units cannot make an assault or counter-charge.
- Cavalry cannot assault Infantry or Artillery defending buildings, or in field works unless the assault is through the rear of such fieldworks.
- Infantry cannot assault *Steady* or *Disordered* enemy Cavalry, even if in the flank or rear.
- Infantry *Skirmishers* cannot assault the front of non-Skirmishers.
- Units cannot assault across a stream or river if the water is shoulder high or a surging torrent.

Russian Grenadier

- The following interpenetrations during an assault are not allowed, other than by *Impetuous* units that have failed a test to not assault:
  - Assaults which pass through Cavalry of any type or command.
  - Assaults which pass through Infantry of a different division unless that Infantry is entirely in Skirmish formation.
  - Assaults which pass through any *Broken* troops other than Artillery.

WHEELING DURING AN ASSAULT MOVE

- Units making an assault move may wheel up to 90 degrees but cannot exceed half their normal move distance in doing so.
- All wheeling must be completed at the start of the assault move before any 'straight ahead' movement is made.
- A unit may only wheel towards their target and must wheel as far as necessary to place some part of the target in front of the centre of their own unit, or as far as possible if this would otherwise cause them to not reach their target.
- They may not wheel to place less of their target to their front or past the point at which the centre of the targets front edge is directly ahead of the centre of their own unit.
- An impetuous unit making an assault may make any legal wheel as necessary to avoid bursting through friends.

REACTION MOVES

A unit that is the target of an assault may perform the following actions:

- Default actions not requiring a *Cohesion Test*:
  - Halt – Infantry not in Square being assaulted by other Infantry.
  - Halt – Infantry in Square being assaulted by Cavalry.
  - Retire if Artillery – unlimbered Artillery will normally be abandoned and the gunners take refuge behind an Infantry unit within 2MU (see *Abandoned Guns*). Limbered Artillery will make a retire move as normal (see *Outcome Moves*).
  - Evade if light Cavalry in *single rank*.

WHEELING DURING A CHARGE

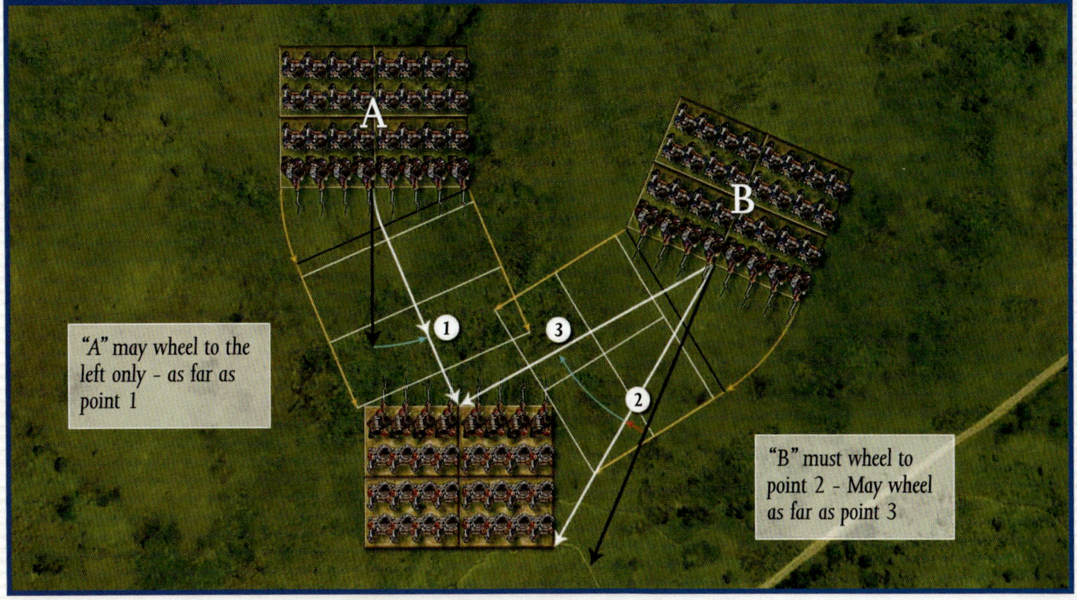
A
B
1
2
3
"A" may wheel to the left only - as far as point 1
"B" must wheel to point 2 - May wheel as far as point 3

- Evade if Infantry *Skirmishers*. They may choose to stand if assaulted by other Infantry *Skirmishers* and MUST evade if assaulted by others. Units passed through take a *Cohesion Test*.
- Counter-charge – If Cavalry are assaulted frontally by other Cavalry. Simply move the non-active player's units towards their attackers, wheeling towards them as far as necessary. The distance of this counter-charge is either 4MU or half the distance between themselves and the assaulting unit, whichever is less (the wheel is 'free'). If they cannot move their full distance, then move them as far as possible – they are still considered to be counter-charging.
- Only *Steady* and *Disordered* Cavalry can counter-charge. Additionally:
  - Light Cavalry *Skirmishers* may only freely counter-charge other light Cavalry *Skirmishers*.
  - Other *Steady* and *Disordered* Cavalry MUST counter-charge.

All retires or evades are conducted according to the rules in the *Outcome Moves* section. If a unit retiring or evading from an assault is contacted by the enemy it automatically drops a cohesion level, regardless of facing and retires an additional 4MU retaining its original facing.

All other actions require a *Cohesion Test* to be taken. Any failure of this test results in the testing unit dropping one level of cohesion.

Actions requiring a compulsory *Cohesion Test*:

- All *Wavering* units must take a *Cohesion Test* if assaulted. If they pass, they will stand or evade as normal. If they fail, they become *Broken* immediately. They automatically fail if the enemy would contact them in the flank or rear. They must test a second time if they stand and also wish to reform.
- Infantry in the open who are neither in Square nor behind an obstacle must take a *Cohesion Test* if being assaulted by Cavalry. The owning player must choose whether or not to form Square and the Infantry always ends in the formation chosen even if the test is failed. It is harder to successfully form Square from Extended Line than from any other formation. *Light infantry* in *Skirmish* formation must evade, they cannot attempt to form Square.
- Infantry units in Square assaulted by enemy Infantry only. They may stay in Square or change to Tactical formation. The unit ends in its chosen formation even if the test is failed.
- Light Cavalry in Skirmish formation must test if they wish to counter-charge non-Skirmishing Cavalry. They will evade if the test is failed.
- Unlimbered Artillery must test if they wish to stand and fire. If the test is failed the guns are abandoned.
- Unlimbered horse Artillery being assaulted by an enemy starting their move from more than 4MU away may choose to limber and retire. The Artillery will make a retire move even if failing the test.
- An unlimbered Artillery unit may attempt to fire at medium range before abandoning guns if the enemy assault starts more than 4MU away. If the enemy assault is stopped by the fire the Artillery will remain where they are and fire again during the following Firing Phase. If the test is failed *foot artillery* units will abandon their guns, while *horse artillery* will limber and retire. (see the *Outcome moves* section)

All failed tests will cause 1 loss in cohesion except that abandoned Artillery units have their own special rules (see *Abandoned Guns*).

French Caisson on the move

EVADE MOVES

An evade move is treated the same as any other retire move, the rules for which are described in *Outcome Moves/Retiring Units*.

The distance of an evade move is as follows:

- Skirmishing Infantry: D6 + 2 MU
- Limbered Foot Artillery: D6 + 2 MU
- Skirmishing light Cavalry: D6 + 4 MU
- Limbered Horse Artillery: D6 + 4 MU
- Unlimbered Horse Artillery: D6 + 2 MU (ending limbered)

If the target of an assault or pursuit moves out of range, then the moving unit may wheel towards the next nearest target which was within 2MU of the original target before it moved, or within 2MU of the path of a retire move. For the purposes of this rule, abandoned Artillery models are ignored. If this new target can be reached as part of a normal assault move it reacts as if it was the original target. If a new target is contacted within the first half move of a pursuit move then a 2nd combat may occur. If this target is contacted after the first half move of a pursuit then combat occurs next turn. If no new target is available the assaulting or pursuing unit completes its full move distance in direction of the original assault or pursuit.

INTERCEPT MOVES

An intercept move may be up to a maximum of 2MU for Infantry and 4MU for Cavalry. At the start of an intercept move, Infantry can wheel up to 1MU and Cavalry up to 2MU forwards if this results in more of the intercepting unit ending its move in front of the assaulting unit. The amount of wheel does not count

INTERCEPTIONS

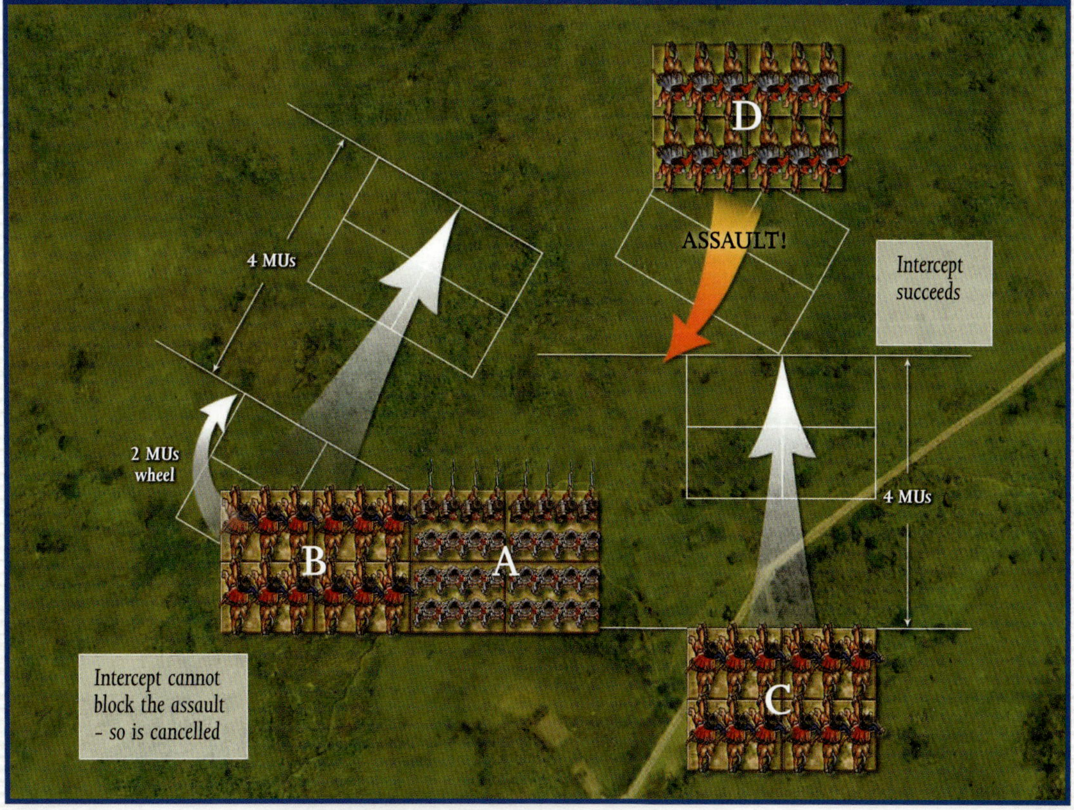

as part of the intercept move distance. If the move does not place the interceptors in a position where they will be contacted by the assaulting unit then the intercept move may not be made. A successful interception is resolved during the Combat Phase.

Only *Steady* and *Disordered* Infantry and Cavalry may intercept, and they may only do so in the following circumstances:

- An intercept move may only be performed by units of Cavalry or Infantry in Tactical formation. Infantry may only intercept other Infantry. Cavalry may intercept any assaulting troops.
- *Steady*, unspent units of Cavalry or Infantry may intercept freely without a CMT.
- *Disordered* or *Spent* units may make an intercept move but must first pass a CMT. However a unit with an attached *Brigade Commander* or led by a *Division Commander* will automatically pass such a CMT. A unit led by a *Corps Commander* may also intercept, but only if he immediately expends all of his remaining *Command Points.*
- No part of an intercept move may cross difficult terrain.
- No part of an intercept move may pass through another friendly unit.
- Unless contacting the enemy flank or rear, the interceptors must move a minimum of 1MU if Infantry or 2MU if Cavalry, or halfway towards the assaulting unit if this is less. The assaulting unit will then move into contact with the interceptors.
- To intercept the flank or rear of an assaulting unit the interceptors must have been in a position to make a legal flank or rear assault and within intercept range before the assaulting unit started its move. The interceptors move into contact with the flank of the assaulting unit, counting this as a normal flank or rear assault. This cancels the assault immediately.

Additionally:

- An Infantry unit being intercepted by Cavalry does not have the option to form Square and will fight intercepting Cavalry in its original formation.
- A unit being intercepted may not be fired upon by the original target of the assault.
- The original target of the assault does not have to make any of the otherwise compulsory tests for being assaulted if all of the assaulting units fail to make contact because of an interception.

DEFENSIVE FIRE

If an Artillery unit is the target of an assault and chooses to fire at medium range before retiring, then the fire effects are calculated at the point when the enemy is furthest away but within 6MU. This may mean that the firing is performed before the enemy unit starts its move. If the enemy is forced to halt, the assault is cancelled at this point.

Other than Artillery firing as above, the only firing allowed during the assault phase is at close range and only at assaulting units. If the unit being assaulted chooses to stand and fire, the assaulting unit must 'pause' 2MU from the target and receive fire at that range. See *Firing Phase.* Firing is calculated as if the assault would complete successfully. This means that some units may fire at assaulting units which do not physically move to within close range.

If the result of firing is *'must pass a CMT to contact or advance'* then the assaulting unit may choose to expend one of its *Division Commander's Command Points* and take a CMT. If the test is passed the assaulting units move into contact. If the test is failed, or the test is not taken they will retire to 3MU if Cavalry or stay at 2MU if Infantry. If the retiring Cavalry has an attachment of Artillery and the only enemy within 2MU is Infantry in Square it may choose to remain at 2MU.

If the result of the firing leaves an assaulting Infantry unit not in contact but within firing range, it will be allowed to fire as normal during the Firing Phase.

DEFENSIVE FIRE

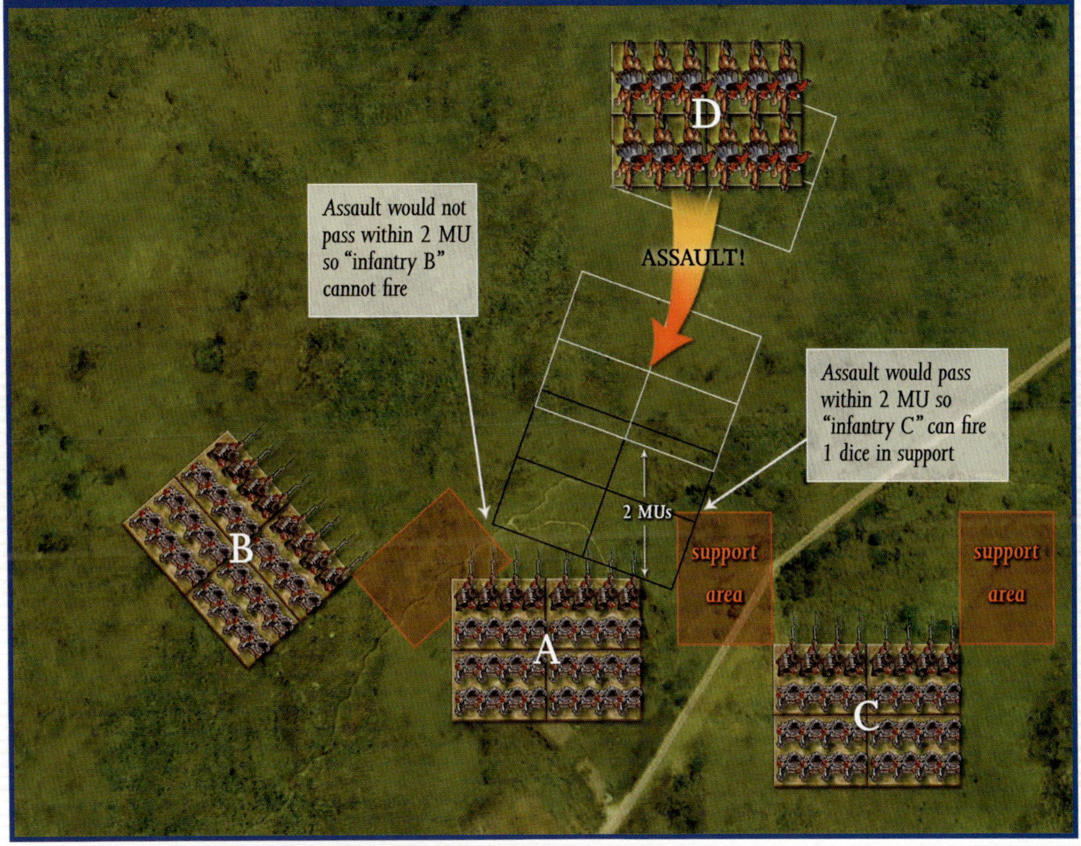
D
ASSAULT!
Assault would not pass within 2 MU so "infantry B" cannot fire
Assault would pass within 2 MU so "infantry C" can fire 1 dice in support
2 MUs
B
support area
A
support area
C

ASSAULTING A FLANK OR REAR

Attacking an enemy in either the flank or rear gives a large bonus to the attackers. To assault or intercept the flank or rear of an enemy a unit must fulfil the following requirements:

- It must not start its move even partially in front of its target.
- It must begin its move with the centre of its front edge behind a line extending the front edge of the target enemy.
- It must contact the enemy flank or rear edge or rear corner with its own front edge or front corner.
- It cannot wheel more than 90 degrees and any wheel must be completed during the first half of the move.

A move that satisfies all of the above is considered to have assaulted the flank or rear of the enemy unit. If there is no other firing that could stop the assault completing, the unit being assaulted drops a level of cohesion BEFORE it can fire defensively at other assaulting units, otherwise it drops a level of cohesion AFTER it has fired any defensive fire. An intercepted unit may not fire defensively. A unit may not fire at enemy units assaulting its flank or rear. If a charge successfully contacts a flank or rear the unit contacted will immediately turn to face the attackers, unless also contacted on another face. It still counts as being attacked in flank or rear for combat purposes.

FLANK AND REAR ASSAULTS

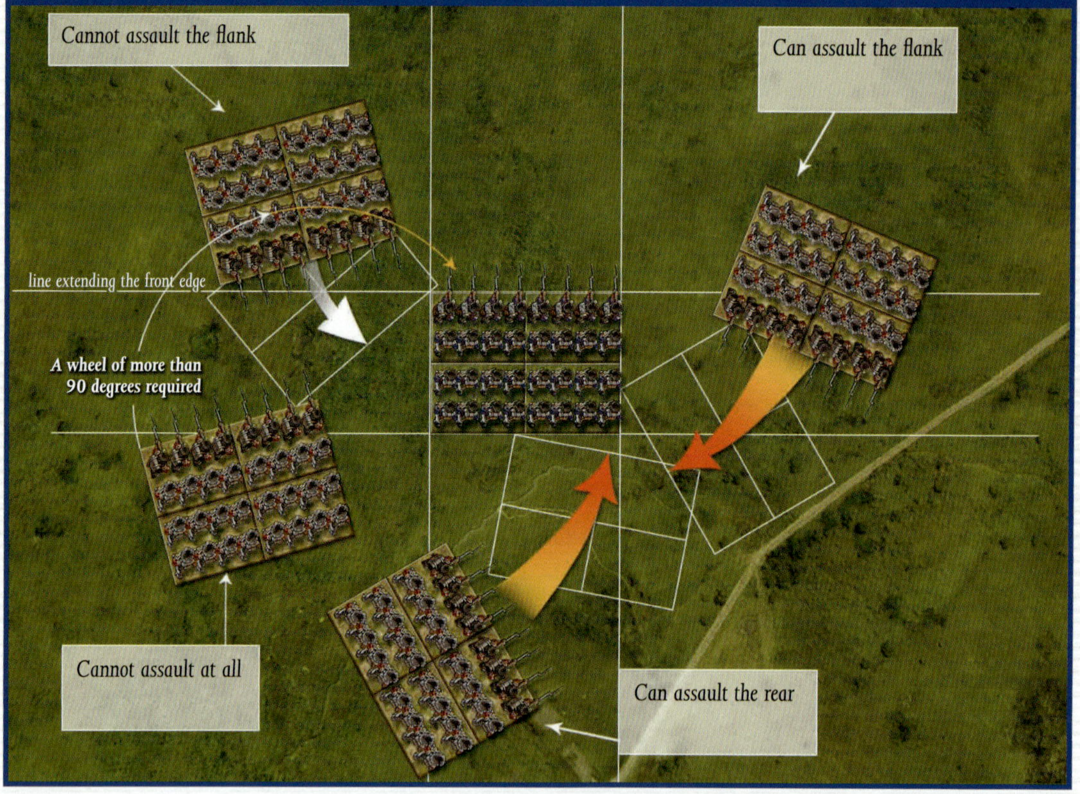

THE MOVEMENT PHASE

RESERVES AND FLANK MARCHES

A reserve is a division that is left off the rear edge of the table. A flank march is a division that is attempting to enter from either side edge of the table.

At the beginning of the Movement Phase and starting with turn 2 the active player MUST try to activate any division that starts off-table either from reserve or flank marching.

The procedure for activating this division is as follows:

- Roll 1 dice for each level of the *Division Commander* (*Competent* = 1 dice, *Skilled* = 2 dice, *Exceptional* = 3 dice). The activation score required is a 5 or higher on any dice.
- If the activation roll is passed the player may start to bring on his reserves at the start of his next Movement Phase. He must tell his opponent which edge (and sector) of the table they are approaching from, and reveal the note defining this approach. If the activation test fails he must test again the following turn.
- If any enemy unit moves to within 12MU of a reserve division's arrival edge and sector the reserves will begin to arrive during the player's next Movement Phase without rolling dice.
- Moving onto the table with reserves or flank marches only occurs during

Polish Voltigeur

the Movement Phase. That is, it may not assault on the move that it enters.

MOVING RESERVES AND FLANK MARCHES ONTO THE TABLE

On the move following activation, units of a reserve or flank march can move onto the table, measuring their move distance from the edge and sector from which they enter.

- Artillery will always enter limbered.
- Infantry and Cavalry can enter the table in any formation except Square.
- The commander of the arriving force must lead the first non-artillery unit placed on the table.
- No unit may move to within 2 MU of an enemy unit on the turn of arrival.
- Arriving units may move along a road if there is one crossing the table edge in that sector.
- An arriving unit that does not move to within 6MU of an enemy unit may attempt a 2nd move as normal.
- Only 3 units may enter the table during the first move of arrival. The remaining units of the division enter during subsequent moves, 3 units per move, without a further test.
- Enemy units within 6MU of the point of entry of an arriving unit, which are not in combat, and not in buildings or field fortifications, must be moved directly away from the edge of arrival to a position 6MU away from it. The moved units are placed in the same formation, facing their nearest enemy (including new arrivals) and take a cohesion loss. If the unit is already *Wavering* it will instead make an *outcome move,* with a minimum distance of 6MU, moving directly away from the arriving unit's table edge. It will not take an additional cohesion loss.
- If a unit due to arrive cannot be placed on the table without being within 2MU of enemy, it is placed with the whole of its rear edge touching the table edge, as long as they can do so without touching the enemy. They cannot move any further. If any unit of a command cannot be placed on the table it must wait until a subsequent move but need not test again for entry.

GENERAL MOVEMENT RULES

During the Movement Phase the active player may move any units that did not move during the Assault Phase, did not enter as reserves or a flank march this move and were not forced to make an outcome move during this turn's assault and Firing Phases. Some moves may not be performed unless the unit passes a *Complex Move Test.*

MOVEMENT ALLOWANCES

The number of MU that a unit may move in a single phase is given in the following table:

MOVEMENT TABLE

Unit type		Open	Rough	Difficult
Unreformed Infantry	In Tactical or Extended Line	4	3	2
Reformed Infantry	In Extended Line	3	2	1
	In Tactical formation	6	4	2
Any Infantry	In March Column	6	4	4
	In Skirmish formation		6	4
Unlimbered Artillery	move by prolong – if any guns are heavy	2	1	N/A
	move by prolong – with no heavy guns		2	1
Limbered Artillery	Foot Artillery	6	4	2
	Horse Artillery	10		
Cavalry	Heavy	8	6	2
	Regular Light unless in single rank	10		4
	In single rank, *Irregular* light or any in March Column		8	6
Corps or *Division Commander* moving on his own				

- Units in March Column and limbered Artillery move double distance if moving entirely on a road, providing they remain outside 6MU of the enemy for the duration of the move.
- Units of Artillery deployed in field fortifications may never be moved, other than to wheel before firing. They must be returned to their original facing during the Recovery Phase.
- With the exception of unlimbered heavy artillery in difficult terrain, all units can move a minimum of 1MU in all terrain and conditions (even Infantry in square).
- A medium artillery unit moves as if heavy if it has been allocated a heavy artillery attachment.
- An artillery unit may unlimber facing any direction.
  - The unlimbered unit must have one of it corners touching the limbered model's original front edge.
  - No part of the unlimbered unit can be further forwards than the front edge of the limbered model.
  - No unlimbered base can be further than 1MU from some part of the original limbered model.
- When an artillery unit changes formation from unlimbered to limbered, the limbered model should be placed in one of 4 possible positions:
  - Facing forwards: In place of one of the unlimbered bases with the front edge and front corners aligned with the original base's front edge and front corners.
  - Facing backwards: In place of one of the unlimbered bases with the rear edge and rear corners aligned with the original base's front edge and front corners.
  - Facing to the right: With its front edge and left front corner aligned with the unlimbered units right edge and right front corner.
  - Facing to the left: With its front edge and right front corner aligned with the unlimbered units left edge and left front corner.

The effect of terrain on the ability of a unit to fire and fight is colour coded in the *Movement Table* as follows:

No disordering effect
Unit fires and fights as if 1 Cohesion level lower
Unit fires and fights as if 2 Cohesion levels lower
N/A = Not allowed

Note that Reformed and Non-reformed Infantry move different distances when in Tactical formation and in Extended Line. This represents the slower rate of movement of those units which still used the linear formations, compared to reformed units which tended to operate in column formations within the Tactical footprint. Our accompanying army list books indicate whether infantry in each national or army list are reformed or unreformed.

TERRAIN EFFECTS

Units positioned in certain types of ***terrain*** can suffer a temporary loss of cohesion, making them function less effectively, especially if they need to stay in formation to be fully effective. *Skirmishers* suffer less as their loose formation permits them to operate effectively in almost any type of terrain.

Terrain can also affect the movement distances of *Brigade Groups*. The *General Movement Rules* section fully details how and where *Brigade Groups* are affected in this way.

Individual units that are in more than one type of terrain are affected by the terrain that reduces their movement most or causes them the most loss of cohesion. However a unit with at least one front rank base, and half its total bases, entirely in the open may fire as 1 cohesion level lower. If such a unit is large, it may instead choose to fire with the dice of a small unit from the bases partially in the open. Troops affected by terrain automatically recover when the unit leaves the terrain that caused the disorder.

MOVING UNITS

Movement is carried out by measuring each corner of the unit to be moved.

Each unit may move any distance up to the maximum allowed in the movement table. Some moves or changes in formation may require that the unit must

FIRING FROM TERRAIN

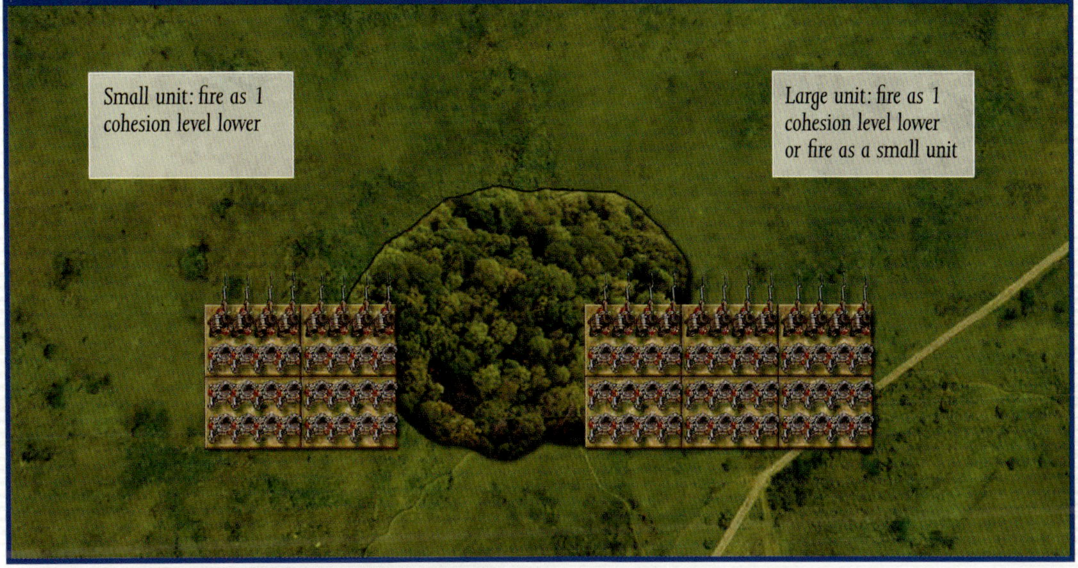
Small unit: fire as 1 cohesion level lower
Large unit: fire as 1 cohesion level lower or fire as a small unit

first pass a CMT. See *the Complex Move Test* section in the Detailed Rules. If the unit always stays more than 6MU from enemy combat units (not commanders) it may also be eligible to make a 2nd move.

Heavy rain or Snow reduces movement by one level. That is, troops in Open terrain move as if in Rough, troops in Rough terrain move as if in Difficult. Units in Difficult terrain in Heavy Rain or Snow have their Difficult movement rate halved, but with a minimum of 1MU.

During the Movement Phase a player may move any or all of his units up to their full movement allowance. Some moves are free, some moves require the taking of a test (see the *Complex Move Test*) and some moves are not allowed.

A *Division Commander* uses his *Command Points* to make complex moves with troops under his command. He must allocate one *Command Point* to each unit within his command range that will perform a *Complex Move Test.* If all of his *Command Points* have been allocated then no further complex moves may be attempted.

Once a unit has determined the type of move it is to perform it will be moved using the following rules:

- Units *Broken* in the opponent's last turn are moved first, using the rules described under *Outcome Moves.* Other units are then moved in any order.
- A unit may move any distance up to the maximum allowed in the *Movement Table.*
- Units in March Column and limbered Artillery may move up to double their normal movement allowance if the entire move is on a road and the unit stays more than 6MU from enemy units (not commanders) throughout the move. Increased movement on roads is allowed even if the road goes through other terrain.
- Infantry units in Skirmish formation and *irregular* light Cavalry may move in any direction up to half the distance allowed in that terrain. They may only do so if their move is more than 2MU from all enemy units (not commanders) throughout.
- Movement is made by an individual unit, by multiple units moving together as a *Brigade Group*, or by commander's bases moving independently.
- When wheeling a unit each front corner is measured. Neither corner may end up more

than its maximum move distance from its original start position. All wheeling must be completed within the first half of the move and before any straight forwards movement if the unit is making an assault move.

- The distance moved cannot exceed the unit's movement allowance in the terrain crossed by any of the unit's bases during any part of the move. Measure the distance between the start position and end position of each front corner.
- Entering and leaving buildings counts as crossing an obstacle. See *Special Features / Buildings* for the full rules.
- A unit cannot wheel through more than 90 degrees in a single move.
- Only Infantry and/or Cavalry units can move into contact with enemy. Contact can only occur voluntarily during the Assault Phase, but may also occur as the result of an outcome move. Units cannot move as a *Brigade Group* when moving into contact with enemy.
- A unit, commander or *Brigade Group* move is over if the player moves, or makes a dice roll for another unit, commander or *Brigade Group*.
- A permitted move of any unit or commander can be taken back and redone, but only if its initial position was marked or can be unambiguously referenced. Otherwise that unit's move is over.
- Any unit making a forwards move or remaining otherwise stationary may make a slide sideways of up to 1 base width.

  The slide will be a *Simple Move* in the following circumstances:

  - The unit makes a forwards move and both front corners move at least 3MU. The unit must remain 6MU from any enemy throughout.
  - The unit makes a forwards move which starts or ends within 6MU of the enemy and the slide is only to avoid friends and is only by the minimum distance necessary. The move cannot start but may end within 2MU of the enemy.

  The slide will be a *Complex Move* in the following circumstance:

  - The unit makes no other move than to slide sideways and is more than 2MU from the enemy throughout. Slides in other circumstances are not permitted.
- A unit may move directly to its rear and end facing forwards or backwards.

All other changes of formation and facing have the following restrictions:

- A unit can turn to face any direction but otherwise remain stationary and in the same formation. This will be a *Complex Move* if

WHEELING DURING A NORMAL MOVE

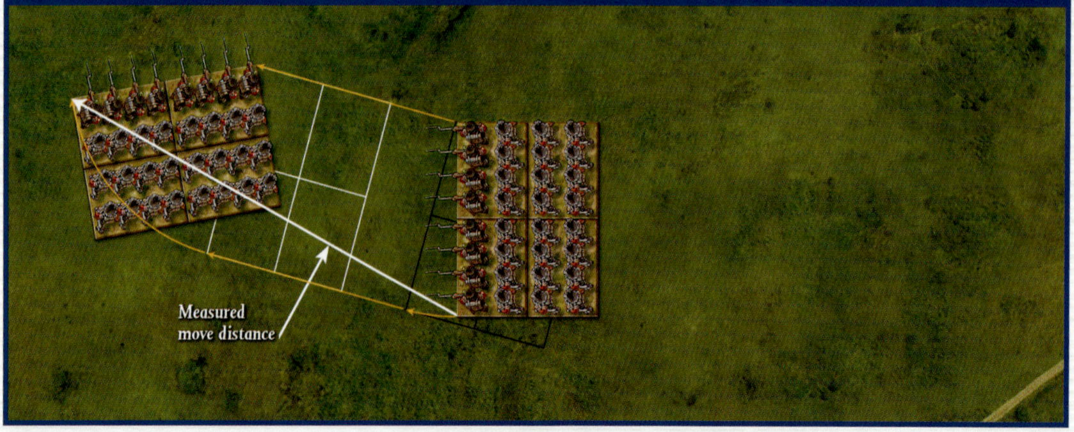

performed by an unlimbered Artillery unit.

- After reforming, the centre point of a unit must be as close as practicable to the same place. A Square may wheel on the spot as part of this reform.
- After reforming, a unit must remain the same distance from the nearest enemy. The reforming unit must slide by the minimum necessary to maintain this distance. If there are 2 enemy units within the same range band, only the nearest one is taken into account (the moving unit's owner selects one if both are equidistant).
- To form Extended Line, the front bases remain stationary, while the rear rank bases are placed level with them. The unit bases can slide sideways to allow placing of the Extended Line, but the original front line must be fully covered by the new position of the bases. If the Extended Line is to be 'kinked', the original front rank bases must remain stationary.
- To reform from Extended Line into Tactical formation, the centre 2 front rank bases must remain stationary, while the other bases are placed behind and lined up with them. This cannot be performed if within 2MU of the front of an enemy unit (not commander).
- A kinked Extended Line moves and takes CMTs with each half-unit independently, but must end the move with all of the unit in a legal formation.
- To form March Column, all bases must be placed behind any one of the original front rank bases. Infantry in Extended Line or Skirmish formation cannot form March Column. They must first form Tactical formation (i.e. taking 2 moves).

REFORMING A UNIT TO FACE A DIFFERENT DIRECTION

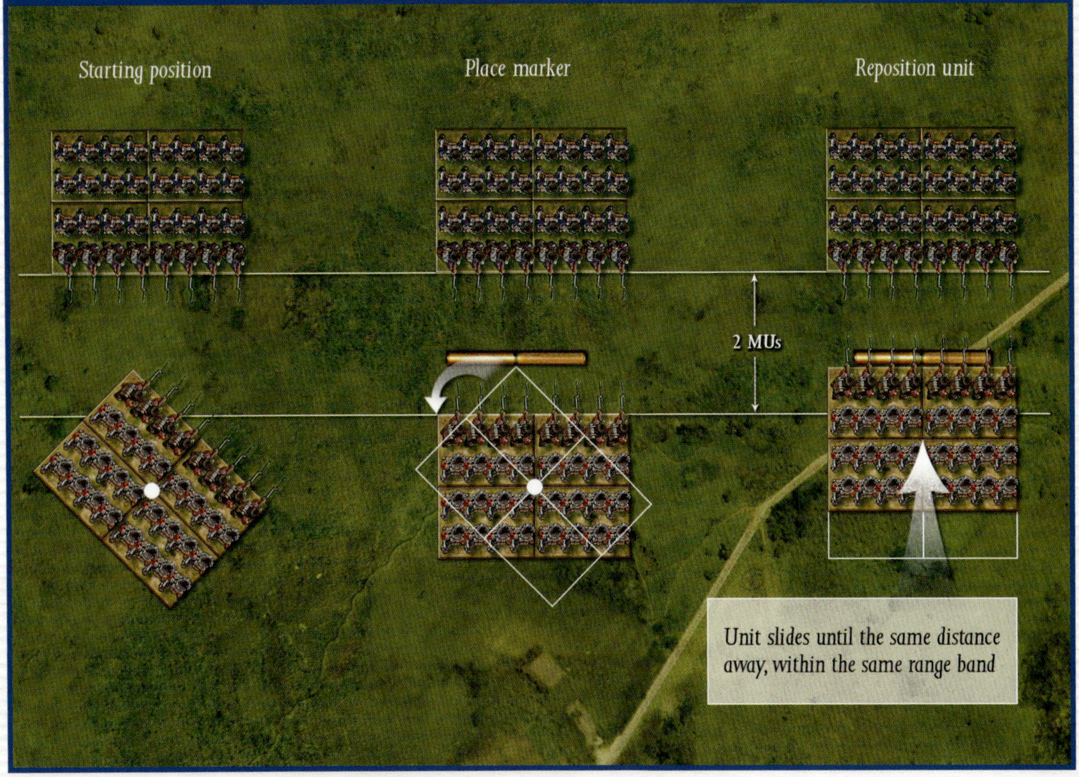
Starting position
Place marker
Reposition unit
2 MUs
Unit slides until the same distance away, within the same range band

- To change from March Column to Tactical formation, the front base of the column becomes one of the front bases of the new formation. A March Column cannot form into Extended Line in one move. It must first reform into Tactical formation (i.e. taking 2 moves).
- A unit in March Column that wheels its front base to change direction will form a kinked column until all its bases pass the point at which it wheeled.

- An Infantry unit can form Square during the Movement Phase taking a full single move unless the unit starts in Skirmish order.
  - If forming Square from Extended Line or March Column the Infantry unit will first place its bases in Tactical formation before turning its rear bases. In the Assault Phase it cannot form Square in a position that takes the unit outside the assault range of the enemy that declared a valid assault upon it. If this would occur, the Square is slid towards the assaulting unit by the minimum necessary to a position just reachable by the assaulting unit.
  - An Infantry unit in Skirmish order takes 2 moves to form Square. It must first change from Skirmish order to any other formation and then form Square the following move.

MOVING THROUGH FRIENDLY UNITS

In certain circumstances units can move voluntarily through other friendly troops, but at other times this may happen involuntarily and may cause deterioration in the cohesion of the unit being passed through.

Interpenetrations are situations where you can choose to move through friendly troops and where there is no penalty for doing so.

The following interpenetrations are permitted:

- Commanders can pass through and be passed through by any troops in any direction.
- Passing through any friendly unit may be performed regardless of facing if either unit is *Skirmishers* or Artillery.
- Any single unit (not *Brigade Group*) can pass through another friendly unit if the unit being passed through remains stationary throughout the movement phase. The moving unit will be required to pass a CMT if it is of a different command to the stationary unit and neither is *Skirmishers* or Artillery.
- Interpenetrations are only permitted if:
  - There is sufficient space beyond the unit passed though.
  - The moving unit can move its front edge (or rear edge if moving backwards) at least half way through the stationary unit. If it can reach this point, then it may move entirely through if there is space beyond without sliding the stationary unit back.
  - If there is insufficient space, then the non-moving unit may slide up to one base depth backwards (or forwards) to make space. If there is still insufficient space, then the move may not be made.
  - The stationary unit is not in March Column.

BRIGADE GROUPS

A **Brigade Group (BG)** is composed of 2 to 4 units plus a leading commander with each in at least partial edge-to-edge contact with another and all facing in the same direction. It can be formed at deployment or during the game by moving units into such a position.

In order to operate as a *Brigade Group* the units forming it must fulfil the following requirements:

- All units must be of the same division.
- No more than one unit may be an Artillery unit.
- It may not include both Infantry and Cavalry units.
- The units forming the brigade group must have their *Division Commander* moving with them who must be with one of the Infantry or Cavalry units in the group.
- The number of units in the group must not exceed the *Division Commander's* command level by more than one. That is, a *Competent*

INTERPENETRATIONS

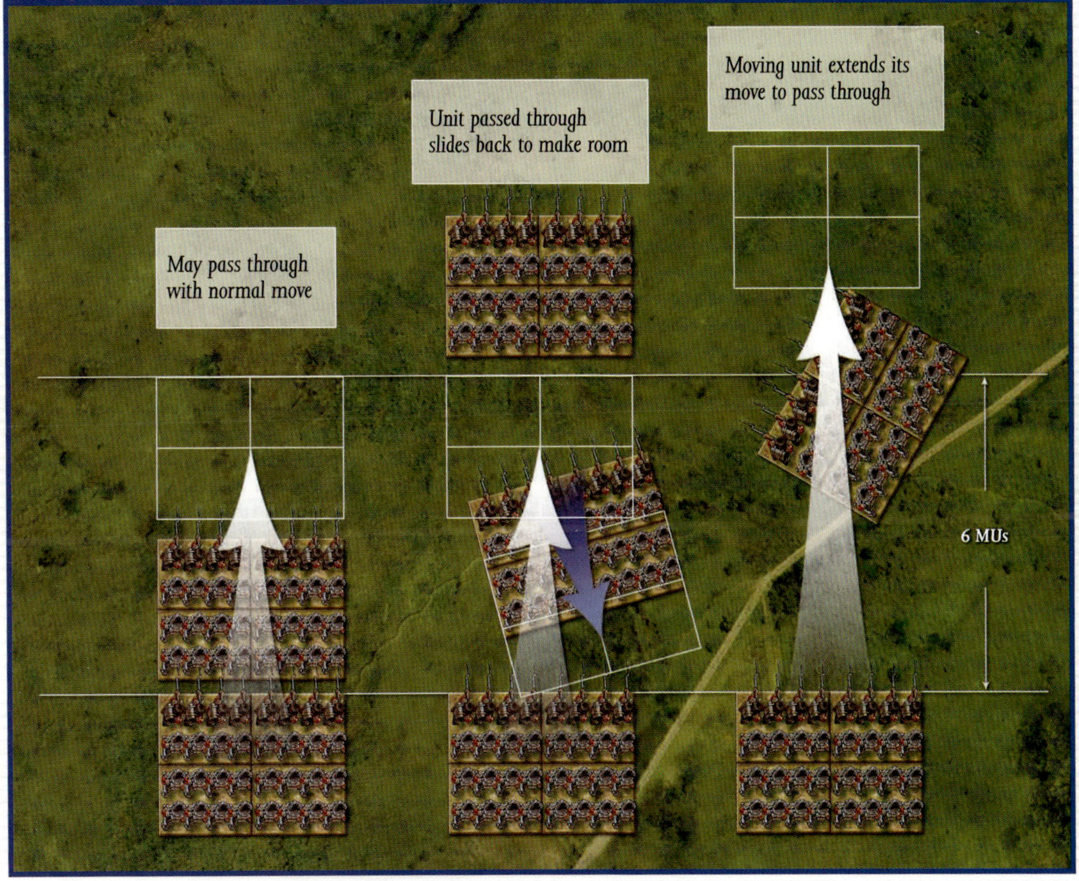
Moving unit extends its move to pass through
Unit passed through slides back to make room
May pass through with normal move
6 MUs

Commander (level1) may control a BG of 2 units, a *Skilled Commander* (level 2) 3 units etc.

- *Wavering* and *Broken* units cannot move as part of a *Brigade Group*.
- No part of a unit forming the *Brigade Group* may be in difficult terrain (even if *Skirmishers*) unless all units are moving in March Column along a road.
- All units of the *Brigade Group* must perform the same action and/or wheel through the same angle except for units moving entirely along and following the path of a road.
- If required to take a CMT, only one *Command Point* is spent and only one dice roll is required. All units in the *Brigade Group* pass or fail as one.
- No turns or changes of formation can be made (except when performing a combined 'move to rear').

The principal advantage of a *Brigade Group* is that it allows multiple units to perform certain actions together and to use a single CMT dice roll for all. If units of different training levels and élan are in the same BG they are all considered to have the lowest training level and lowest élan level of any of the units in the BG.

For example, if a BG is formed of 1 unit of *Superior Conscripts* and 1 unit of *Poor Veterans*, they would both roll dice as *Poor Conscripts*.

The term *Brigade Group* is used for this formation even though the units of such a group may not

FORMING BRIGADE GROUPS

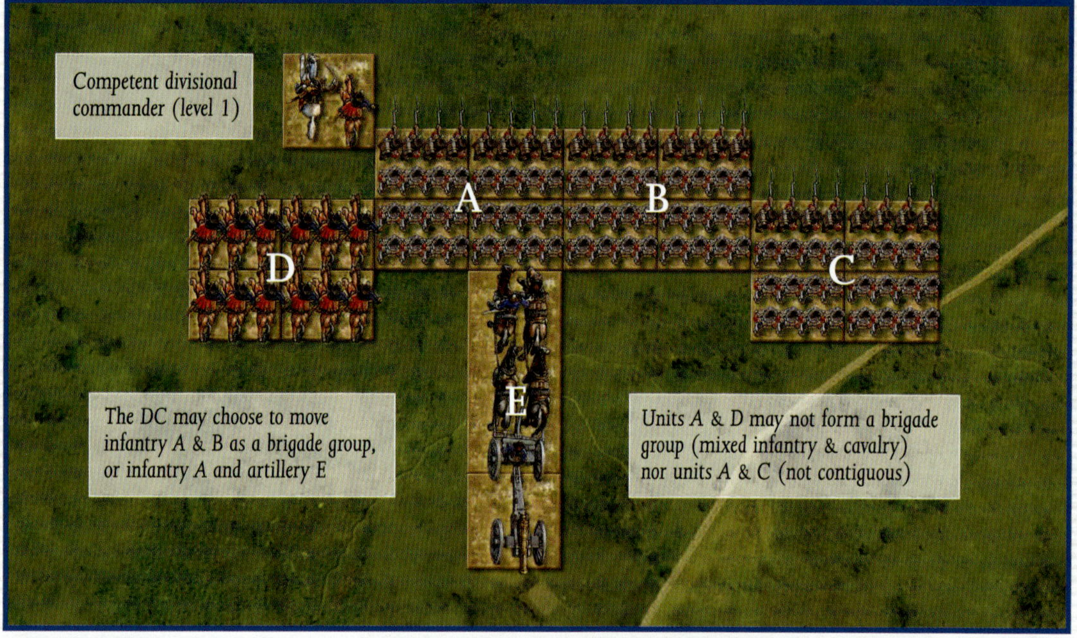
Competent divisional commander (level 1)
A
B
C
D
E
The DC may choose to move infantry A & B as a brigade group, or infantry A and artillery E
Units A & D may not form a brigade group (mixed infantry & cavalry) nor units A & C (not contiguous)

necessarily be part of the same brigade. Players may form a *Brigade Group* with different units in the same battle. The term 'Brigade Group' is used for ease of reference. Players who prefer to record and use historical, or predefined brigade formations, may optionally restrict such formations to units of the same brigade.

EFFECTS OF COHESION LOSSES ON MOVEMENT

A *Disordered* unit must pass a CMT to:

- Advance to within 2MU of an enemy unit.
- Declare an assault on enemy units unless:
  - All of the targets are *Wavering* or *Broken* or presenting their flank or rear.
  - The unit is *Guard, shock cavalry*, or if they are unspent *Impetuous* troops.
  - Counter-charges do not require a test.
- Intercept an enemy assault move without expending a *Command Point*, unless led by a *Division* or *Brigade Commander*.

A *Wavering* unit must:

- Not move to or within 6MU of an enemy unit nor move closer to any enemy already at or within 6MU.
- Take a *Cohesion Test* if assaulted.
- Make an outcome move instead of dropping a cohesion level from shooting if none of the shooting is at close range (even if the close range shooting does not cause a hit).
- Become *Broken* if dropping another cohesion level from any cause.

MOVEMENT OF COMMANDERS

- A *Corps Commander* may only move voluntarily by expending one of his own *Command Points* except during the *Recovery Phase*.
- A *Division Commander* can move in any direction without a CMT and without having to wheel or turn the base to face the direction of movement. He moves the same distance and with the same restriction as *Irregular* light Cavalry.

- A commander base represents the commander and a few aides. They therefore do not obstruct the movement of other troops. Commanders can interpenetrate any friendly troops in any direction and can be passed through by friendly troops in any direction. If he is contacted by enemy units while on his own, he must move to the nearest friendly unit within 10MU. If there is no unit within 10MU then he is considered lost (captured). If he begins the shooting phase on his own and within close or medium range of enemy capable of firing at him, he immediately moves to the nearest friendly unit. A *Corps Commander* forced to move must lose one of his *Command Points* if he has any remaining.
- A Commander may not move on his own within 2MU of the front of an enemy unit, unless he maintains edge contact with one of his own units throughout.
- A commander may join a single unit during the *Movement Phase* or the *Recovery Phase*. The following rules apply:
  - He can only join a single unit of either Infantry or Cavalry. If possible, he must be placed in edge contact with a base of the unit in a position that makes it clear which unit he is with. If not, the player must declare which unit he is with.
  - If he moves with the unit, he must remain with the unit throughout and must remain in exactly the same position relative to it, unless its formation changes. In that case he moves the minimum necessary to a new permitted position. His base can be moved at any time the minimum necessary to a new position if this is necessary to avoid obstructions or make way for friendly or enemy troops. If there is no room left for him to be so placed, a marker must be placed on top of one of the bases of the unit to represent his position.
- To move with a *Brigade Group* a commander must start and end in at least partial edge contact with one of the units and all units of the *Brigade Group* must be within 8MU throughout.
- The unit or *Brigade Group* making a move led by a *Division Commander* does not expend a *Command Point* to attempt a complex move if he remains with the unit or *Brigade Group* throughout. Only a *Division Commander* may move with a *Brigade Group*, which can only contain units of his own command.
- A *Brigade Commander* provides a *Command Point* that may only be used for the unit he is attached to.
- A *Corps Commander* must expend a *Command Point* if a unit he is with performs any action, other than turning or reforming whilst otherwise remaining stationary.

The Old Guard 'En Avant'

- A commander cannot expend *Command Points* whilst the unit he is with is in contact with enemy.
- A *Division Commander's* base is only a marker while his command is off table. It may not move or be attacked until at least one unit of his command is on table.
- Commanders of both players may move up to 4MU at the start of the Recovery Phase. A *Corps Commander* does not expend a *Command Point* to make this move.

COMPLEX MOVE TESTS

Some moves and changes in formation are more complicated than others and require more training to perform. To simulate this we identify these moves as *complex*. In order to perform these manoeuvres a unit must take a **Complex Move Test (CMT)**.

This test is used whenever a unit makes any of the following moves or formation changes:

- Any manoeuvre or formation change listed on the complex move table as requiring a test.
- Any unit responding to an assault being declared upon it as listed in the table.
- Any other allowed move, manoeuvre or formation change not listed as simple.

The table is split into 2 sections – one for actions only occurring during the Assault Phase and one for normal movement actions.

<table>
<tr><th colspan="3">ASSAULT PHASE ONLY</th></tr>
<tr><th>Activity</th><th>Steady or Disordered</th><th>Wavering</th></tr>
<tr><td>Assault through friends who are not Skirmishers, Artillery or part of the same division</td><td rowspan="4">Complex</td><td rowspan="7">N/A</td></tr>
<tr><td>Cavalry assaulting a target also being assaulted by Infantry</td></tr>
<tr><td>Mounted Skirmishers assaulting the front of Steady or Disordered non-Skirmishers.</td></tr>
<tr><td>Assaulting when Disordered or Spent with units that are not Guard, Shock or Impetuous</td></tr>
<tr><td>Any other assault declaration by a unit in command range</td><td>Simple</td></tr>
<tr><td>Impetuous Cavalry ordered not to assault when in assault reach</td><td rowspan="2">Complex</td></tr>
<tr><td>Any attempt to assault when out of command range</td></tr>
<tr><td>Counter-charge if Cavalry</td><td rowspan="2">Simple</td><td rowspan="4">N/A</td></tr>
<tr><td>Make an intercept move if Steady</td></tr>
<tr><td>Make an intercept move if Disordered or Spent</td><td rowspan="2">Complex</td></tr>
<tr><td>Continue into contact after receiving 1 or 2 hits during a charge</td></tr>
</table>

<table>
<tr><th colspan="5">MOVEMENT PHASE ONLY</th></tr>
<tr><th colspan="3">Activity</th><th>Steady or Disordered</th><th>Wavering</th></tr>
<tr><td colspan="3">Activating an off-table command</td><td>Complex</td><td>N/A</td></tr>
<tr><td colspan="3">Any forwards move including a wheel with no change of formation</td><td rowspan="3">Simple</td><td rowspan="2">Simple</td></tr>
<tr><td colspan="3">Turn or wheel to face enemy within 2MU</td></tr>
<tr><td colspan="2" rowspan="2">A change of formation or facing while otherwise stationary</td><td>> 2MU from enemy</td><td>Complex</td></tr>
<tr><td><= 2MU of enemy</td><td rowspan="2">Complex</td><td rowspan="2">N/A</td></tr>
<tr><td colspan="3">Slide 1 base sideways if otherwise stationary and over 2MU from enemy</td></tr>
<tr><td rowspan="3">Pass through friends in any direction</td><td colspan="2">Either unit is Skirmishers or Artillery</td><td rowspan="2">Simple</td><td>Simple</td></tr>
<tr><td colspan="2">If both units of same command</td><td rowspan="2">Complex</td></tr>
<tr><td colspan="2">If units are of different commands</td><td>Complex</td></tr>
<tr><td rowspan="3">Move including 180deg turn before and/or after</td><td>Up to a full move in Line or March Column</td><td>End facing original rear</td><td rowspan="2">Complex</td><td rowspan="2">Complex</td></tr>
<tr><td>1/2 move in any formation</td><td rowspan="2">End facing original front or rear</td></tr>
<tr><td>Up to a full move if Skirmishers</td><td>Simple</td><td>Simple</td></tr>
<tr><td colspan="3">Skirmishers moving 1/2 distance in any direction if outside 2MU</td><td rowspan="2">Simple</td><td rowspan="2">Simple</td></tr>
<tr><td colspan="2" rowspan="2">Crossing obstacle or entering buildings forwards or backwards</td><td>Skirmishers</td></tr>
<tr><td>Non-Skirmishers</td><td>Complex</td><td>Complex</td></tr>
<tr><td rowspan="4">Artillery only</td><td colspan="2">Unlimber</td><td></td><td>N/A</td></tr>
<tr><td colspan="2">Move by prolong forwards or backwards</td><td rowspan="2">Complex</td><td rowspan="3">Complex</td></tr>
<tr><td rowspan="2">Limber</td><td>Heavy Artillery</td></tr>
<tr><td>Medium Artillery</td><td>Simple</td></tr>
<tr><td colspan="3">2nd move if over 6MU from enemy throughout</td><td>Complex</td><td>N/A</td></tr>
</table>

EFFECT OF COMMANDERS ON THE CMT

The skill level of a *Division Commander* affects Complex Move Tests (CMTs) as follows:

Depending on his skill level a *Division Commander* will enable one or more of his units within command range to attempt to pass a CMT. He expends one *Command Point* for each CMT attempted. Multiple CMTs may be attempted by a single unit if *Command Points* are remaining, however, if any CMT is failed, no further CMTs may be taken by that unit during the same phase.

A unit of Infantry or Cavalry led by a commander of any type, and an artillery unit led by a *Brigade Commander*, does not require a *Command Point* for the first CMT taken in any phase. Additional CMTs are rolled for as normal except that they are passed on a 4+ instead of the normal 5+. The commander must remain with the unit throughout the phase for this to apply.

A *Corps Commander* may have to expend a *Command Point* if his base moves other than reforming with a unit. See the *Command Allocation Phase* section for detailed explanations of how and when *Command Points* are spent.

Once a *Division Commander* has expended all of his *Command*

Archduke Charles

Points, no other unit of his command may perform an action requiring a CMT, unless that unit is led by a *Corps Commander* who has unspent *Command Points* or by a *Brigade Commander*.

Players who feel they may lose track of *Command Points* used may use additional counters, or Aide-de-camp (ADC) figures to represent these *Command Points*. The counters may then be moved to the units to which they are allocated and removed once used. A *Division Commander* may make a CMT for a unit outside his command range, but that unit will require one additional *Command Point*.

- A Complex move requires a *CP* unless it is the first CMT taken this phase for a unit led by a commander.
- A unit must successfully complete its 1st move before the CMT for a 2nd move is taken.
- Any move may include a slide sideways up to 1 base width if > 6MU from enemy throughout, or to avoid friends if closer. If the unit is otherwise stationary it will require a CMT.
- A *Wavering* unit may not move to within 10MU of an enemy unit, or closer to any enemy if already within 10MU.

	Type of move	Score required	Commander leading	In command	Out of command
Score required to pass a CMT	Simple	Auto	Auto	No CP required	
	Complex	5+	4+	1 CP required	2 CPs required
	N/A	Not allowed - Unit cannot perform this action			
Re-rolls	Superior:		Guards:	Superior Guards:	Poor:
	Re-roll 1's		Re-roll 1's	Re-roll 1's and 2's	Re-roll 6's

PROCEDURE

A *Complex Move Test* (CMT) must be taken by any unit performing an action on the CMT table listed as 'Complex'. A move indicated as 'Not Allowed' (N/A) cannot be performed even if the unit is led by a commander.

Each unit rolls 1, 2 or 3 dice depending on their training:

- Veterans: 3 dice
- Drilled: 2 dice
- Conscripts: 1 dice
- Irregulars: 1 dice

In addition, units may (or must) re-roll some of their dice depending on the result and their Élan:

- Superior Guard: may re-roll all 1's and 2's if they fail their test.
- Superior troops: may re-roll all 1's if they fail their test.
- Guard: may re-roll all 1's if they fail their test.
- Poor troops: must re-roll all 6's if they pass their test.

The test is successful if at least ONE of the dice scores equal to or above the required number. If ALL dice rolled (after re-rolls) are LESS than the required number the test is failed. If the test is failed the unit may not perform such a move. No loss of cohesion is incurred as a result of this failure.

POINTS TO NOTE ON THE CMT

- A unit can choose not to make a move that requires a CMT.
- If a unit or *Brigade Group* fails its CMT, it can still make a simple move.
- Once the dice have been rolled, that unit or *Brigade Group* must make its move, if any, before others are moved or tested. It is not permitted to conditionally make or change a move depending on the result of a subsequent unit's test.
- A *Division Commander* must expend 1 *Command Point* for each unit attempting a complex move unless it is the first CMT taken that phase for a unit he is leading.
- The position of a unit before movement is used when checking if it is within the command

range of its *Division Commander*. It does not re-measure if it makes a 2nd move.

- If a commander is with a unit or *Brigade Group* when it takes a CMT, he must remain with the same unit for the rest of the phase.
- A mixed *Brigade Group* tests using the number of dice applicable for the unit with the lowest level of training.
- Élan re-rolls apply to the CMT. When testing a *Brigade Group*, its élan is that of the unit with the lowest élan level.
- A unit cannot make a double move if the first move is complex and the CMT is failed.

ABANDONED GUNS

Once an Artillery battery has been abandoned, it may be recovered by returning artillerymen. However, this is not guaranteed. The artillerymen may have been killed, or be dispersed beyond return, or the guns may have been rendered useless by the enemy. To indicate that Artillery has been abandoned but not destroyed, turn one of the bases to face inwards.

Whenever artillerymen leave their guns, they automatically lose cohesion levels. This is in addition to any previous cohesion losses. Cohesion losses are taken as soon as the gunners abandon their guns as follows:

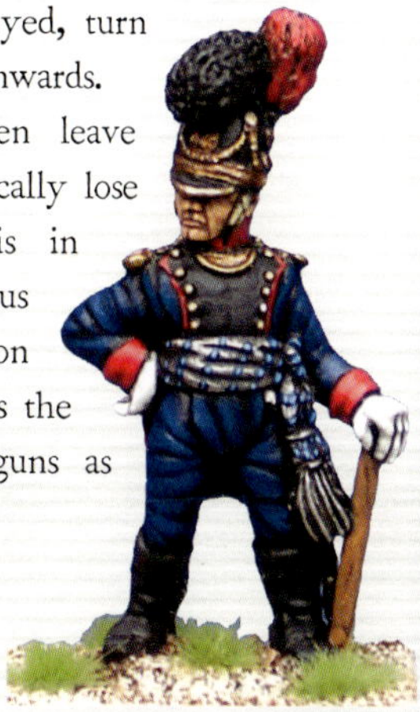

Bavarian Artillery Officer

ABANDONED GUNS

Action forcing abandonment (of unlimbered Artillery):			Cohesion losses
Voluntarily retire to Infantry unit within 2MU when assaulted			-1 cohesion
Otherwise:	If forced to retire by failing a test	Retire from an Infantry assault	-1 cohesion
Otherwise:	If forced to retire by failing a test	Retire from a Cavalry assault	-2 cohesion
Otherwise:	Retire as an outcome move from combat		-2 cohesion
Additional loss if all friends within 2MU retire (once only)			-1 cohesion

If all friends within 2MU are forced to retire to over 2MU while the guns are still abandoned, the guns take an addition cohesion loss due to the gunners being forced to retire with them. The gunners themselves do not require marking and do not exist as a separate unit. All that exists is their ability to recover the guns, which is recorded by the cohesion level of the abandoned battery.

Destroyed French Cannon

An abandoned Artillery unit which accumulates more than 3 cohesion losses is destroyed and removed from the table. Abandoned Artillery never take a *Cohesion Test* other than the single test to recover them. Abandoned Artillery count as lost for victory point purposes until they are recovered.

RECOVERING GUNS

To recover guns the following circumstance must occur:

- The guns must not be within 2MU of an enemy unit.
- There must be a friendly Infantry unit within 6MU.
- The friendly Infantry unit must be closer to the guns than the nearest non-*Broken* enemy unit.

If, at the start of a player's Recovery Phase, the above circumstances have been met, then an attempt to recover the guns MUST be made. This is achieved by passing a cohesion (recovery) test using the normal number of dice for their training level. However, since commanders cannot affect the condition of the guns, the test will be:

- Artillery unit has 2 cohesion losses or less: 5+
- Artillery unit has 3 cohesion losses: 6

Recovered Artillery are automatically marked as *Wavering* and further recovery of cohesion is made as normal. If the test fails the Artillery unit is considered destroyed and removed from the table.

THE FIRING PHASE

During this phase both players may fire any and all units eligible to fire. The active player fires all of his units first and completes all firing effects before the non-active player fires his units. This procedure is also used for defensive fire by the non-active player during the Assault Phase.

UNITS ALLOWED TO FIRE

In order to fire, a unit must fulfil the following requirements:

- It must be an Infantry unit, an Artillery unit or an Artillery attachment.
- It must have an enemy target within range.
- It must not have changed formation or retired as a reaction to an assault earlier this move.

A unit is still allowed to fire if it attempted to assault an enemy unit during the Assault Phase but failed to contact due to enemy fire. A unit which fired defensively in the Assault Phase may fire again in this phase.

A base of a unit cannot fire or be fired upon if it is in contact with an enemy unit, or if it is another base of the same unit adjacent to and touching such a base (even if only corner to corner). Note that bases of a small unit (in Tactical or Square) may never fire or be targeted if any part of the unit is in contact with the enemy. Dice allowance and range is calculated against the permitted target bases only.

FIRING RANGES

Different weapons have different ranges which are defined in the table below:

Unit type	Close	Medium	Long
Unreformed Infantry	2MU	-	-
Reformed and Light Infantry	2MU	6MU	-
Artillery canister	2MU	6MU	-
Artillery round shot	2MU	6MU	16MU
Howitzers	2MU	6MU	16MU
Rockets/Mortars	N/A	N/A	16MU

Units of mortars may not fire at targets if they are even partially within 6MU. Rocket attachments may not add dice to its parent body at close or medium ranges. Use the shortest distance between any point of

British Rocket Battery in action

the firing unit and the target when calculating range. Targets in Extended Line count each half as a separate unit when measuring ranges. An Artillery attachment fires as if lined up with the front rank of its parent unit. For details on how to calculate fire and its effects see *The Firing Mechanism* and *Outcome Moves*.

THE FIRING MECHANISM

During the Firing Phase close range firing is mandatory, medium or long range firing is optional. The firing unit must be able to draw a line from the centre of its front rank to any part of the target unit. No unit may fire through a gap of less than 1 base width (60mm/40mm/30mm).

PROCEDURE

1. Calculate the total number of firing dice available for each unit.
2. Reduce this total due to the effects of cohesion losses.
3. Allocate the remaining dice against available targets.
4. Roll for hits against each target.
5. Apply result to targets and make *Outcome Moves* if required.

DICE AVAILABILITY

Each unit will fire the number of dice as indicated in the following tables:

Units firing at CLOSE RANGE (2MU or less):

CLOSE (musket) range:		0 to 2 MU
Unit Type	**Small unit**	**Large Unit**
Infantry in Tactical	4	6
Each 1/2 of Ext Line		
Artillery * (not mortars)	6	8
Square or *Skirmishers*	3	4
Artillery attachment **	+2 dice	
Square with art att.	+1 dice	
Supporting unit - Infantry	+1 dice	
Supporting unit - Artillery	+2 dice	
* Mortars may not fire at close range ** Attachments of rockets may not add dice to close range firing.		

Units firing at MEDIUM RANGE (over 2MU to 6MU):

MEDIUM (Skirmishing/canister) **Range:**		2 to 6 MU
Unit Type	**Small unit**	**Large Unit**
Non-reformed Infantry	0	0
Non-reformed + skirm. att.	3	4
Reformed line Infantry		
Reformed + skirm. att.	4	5
Light Infantry	5	6
Artillery (except mortars) *	6	8
Artillery attachment **	+2 dice for a unit with no skirmishers	
	+1 dice otherwise	
Enemy Cavalry in 6MU	-1 dice if rifles, -2 dice if muskets	
* Mortars may not fire at medium range. ** Artillery attachments add dice at medium range as follows: • Attachments of rockets may not add dice to medium range firing. • Artillery attached to a unit of unreformed Infantry with no *Skirmishers*, or attached to any Cavalry unit fires with 2 dice. • Artillery attached to a unit that has its own dice at medium range adds 1 dice. • Artillery attachments cannot add dice at medium range to the fire of a unit entirely in Skirmish formation.		

Artillery units firing at LONG RANGE (over 6MU to 16MU):

LONG (round shot) **Range:**		6 to 16 MU
Unit Type	**Small unit**	**Large Unit**
Mortars & Heavy artillery	4	5
Medium artillery	3	4
Artillery attachment	+1 dice	

To calculate the number of dice used by each unit:

- Select the appropriate range table (Close, Medium or Long). Cross-reference the unit type and formation against the size of the unit to determine the starting number of dice.
- Add 1 or 2 dice if the unit has an Artillery attachment - unless the parent body is *light*

Russian Infantry

infantry entirely in Skirmish formation, in which case the attached Artillery base does not fire.

- Add 1 or 2 dice for adjacent units in support (see *Supporting Fire*).
- Infantry in Square can only fire at close range.
- Units in March Column cannot fire or add supporting dice to another unit.

EFFECTS OF ENEMY CAVALRY

Skirmishers would rarely operate far from the parent body when under threat from enemy Cavalry. So enemy Cavalry within 6MU affects Infantry firing in the following circumstances:

- If the enemy Cavalry is a separate unit.
- If the Cavalry is an attachment to any enemy Infantry unit that is even partially the target of the firing unit.
- If any part of the firing Infantry unit carries rifles, or if it has an attachment armed with rifles, it loses 1 dice. Otherwise it loses 2 dice.

Note that enemy cavalry have no effect on the firing of Artillery units (including attachments).

EFFECTS OF COHESION LOSSES ON FIRING

If a unit has lost levels of cohesion, is affected by *Poor* weather, or is non-*Skirmishers* in unfavourable terrain, then the number of dice rolled is reduced as follows:

- A unit with 1 cohesion loss (or *Disordered*) (or *Steady* and *Spent*) loses 1 dice for each full group of 3 dice.

French 5th Hussars

- A unit with 2 cohesion losses (or *Wavering*) loses 1 dice for each 2 dice.
- A unit with 3 cohesion losses (or *Broken*) cannot fire.
- Infantry and Artillery in either snow or rain fire as 1 cohesion level lower unless the firers are in buildings.

For example: A unit that would normally have 5 dice would lose 1 if *Disordered* and 2 if *Wavering*. A *Wavering* non-*Skirmishing* unit in rough terrain could not fire.

EXTENDED LINE

An Infantry unit in Extended Line has slightly different rules as follows:

- A unit in Extended Line fires at close range as 2 adjacent half units, each with its own centre point (when determining targets). Each half calculates its own number of dice as if it was a complete unit, even if in Skirmish order.
- An Artillery attachment adds its bonus dice to the half unit in which the attachment is placed.
- Each half may receive bonus dice from their own valid supporting units, which could include its other half.

SUPPORTING FIRE

Normally a unit can only fire at a unit directly to their front. However, there are times when a unit can provide supporting fire at close range for a unit adjacent to and within a base depth of it. This is defined by the following rule:

If a unit has no other target this phase and there is an enemy target forwards of its front line and also within one base width of its side edge, it may add extra dice to the fire of the friendly unit which is firing at it. This extra dice will use the To-hit value of the supported friendly unit.

A *Wavering* or *Broken* unit cannot provide supporting fire. A unit can only add supporting dice to the fire of another unit. A unit in Extended Line firing with half its frontage (as a single unit) may benefit from the supporting fire of its other half unit. A unit can only receive additional supporting fire from a single friendly unit on each flank.

The supporting unit will add 2 dice if it is an Artillery unit, or is an Infantry unit with Artillery attachment. It will add 1 dice if it is Infantry without an Artillery attachment. If more than one support target is in range, it will add its fire against the nearest target. The firing player chooses the target if 2 are equidistant.

IDENTIFYING TARGETS

Artillery and Infantry can fire at any target straight ahead, however an Artillery unit may pivot first. This is to simulate the greater arc of fire that an Artillery piece has. The Artillery unit pivots by moving any one of its corners up to 1MU forwards or backwards. This move may not be used to reduce or extend the range band at which the Artillery unit started or to move it to a different range band of enemy capable of firing at it. An artillery unit cannot pivot to provide supporting fire.

DICE ALLOCATION

Dice must be allocated against enemy targets using the following target priorities:

- Artillery will always direct all their fire at targets within the closest range band.
- A unit must allocate maximum dice at a close range target before any are allocated to a medium range target.
- Artillery may ignore units entirely in Skirmish formation if another target is available in the same range band.
- No unit may fire at a target if a line cannot be drawn from the centre of the firing unit to any part of the target.
- The firers will fire as if 1 cohesion level lower if a line cannot be drawn from both its front corners to a target unit.
- A large unit will fire as if a small unit if the target is only to the front of one 'end' base (one base width).

FIRING RANGES

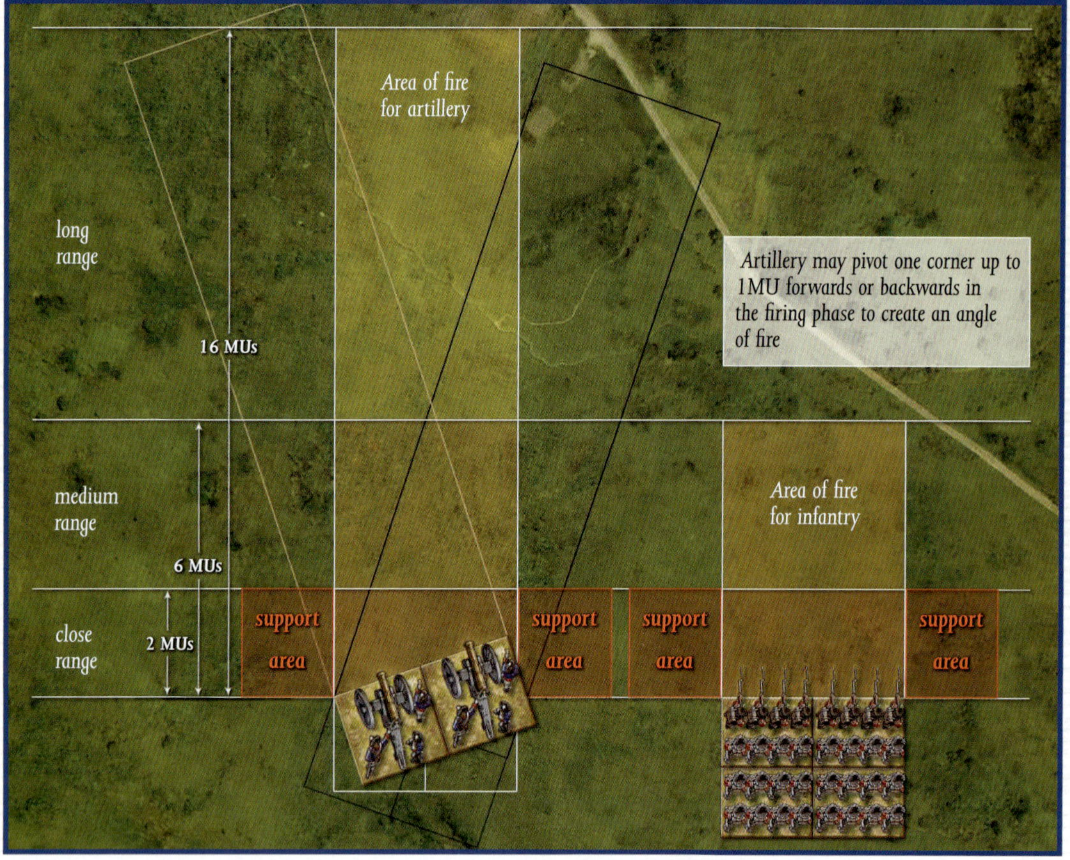

SPLITTING FIRE BETWEEN MULTIPLE TARGETS

- Every target in arc in the closest range band must be allocated at least 1 dice if 5 or less dice are available and 2 dice if 6 or more dice are available.
- Extra dice are allocated at targets in the range band as the player wishes. All dice allocation against a single target must to be made before any dice are rolled.
- If there are more targets in the range band than available dice, the player chooses which targets to fire at, but no target can have more than 1 die.
- The unit most central to the target area must receive at least as many dice as any other target.

FIRING OVER INTERVENING UNITS

Firing over other units was rare during this period. When it did occur, it did not involve batteries of the size and make-up represented by the units in these rules. Artillery attachments could be assumed to be firing overhead where circumstances permit, but as a general rule no firing over other units is permitted.

Artillery is allowed to fire through enemy *Skirmishers* at valid targets beyond; as long as the target is at long range, the *Skirmishers* are nearer to the guns than the target and the *Skirmishers* are at least 2MU away from both.

THE TO-HIT SCORE

The To-hit score required for each dice rolled is shown on the following table:

MULTI-UNIT FIRE

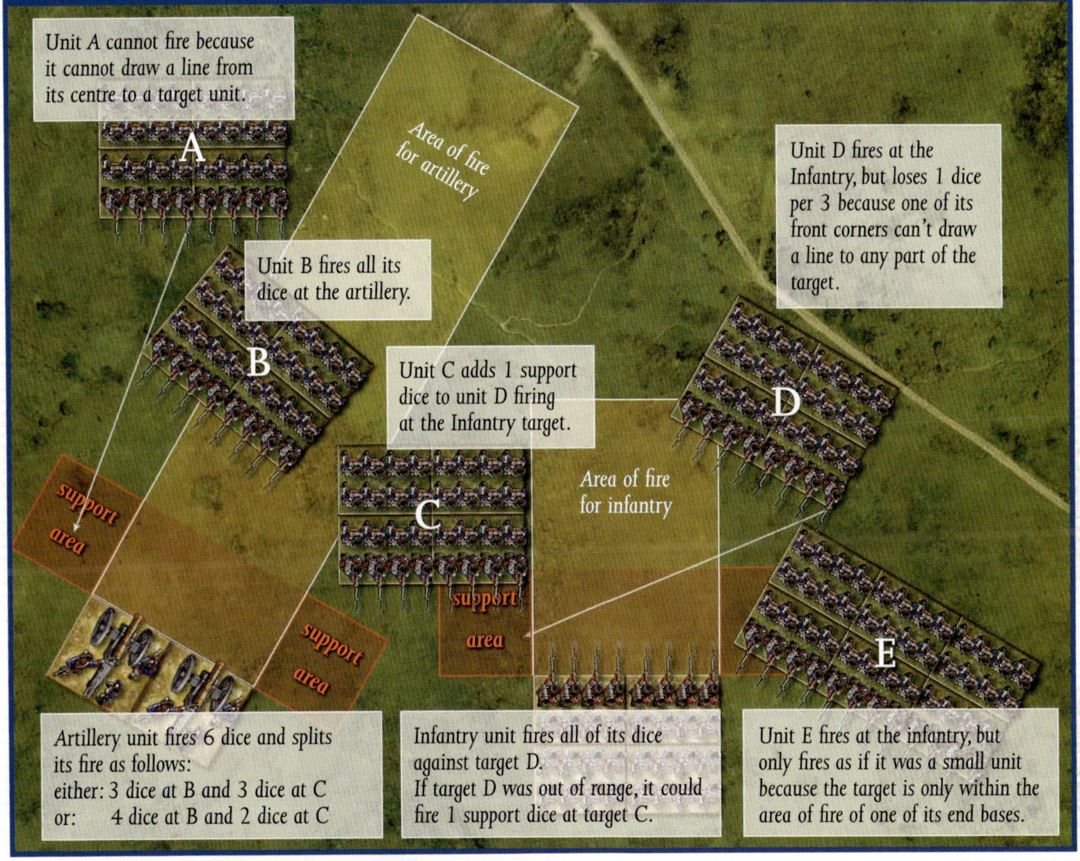

Unit A cannot fire because it cannot draw a line from its centre to a target unit.
A
Area of fire for artillery
Unit B fires all its dice at the artillery.
B
Unit D fires at the Infantry, but loses 1 dice per 3 because one of its front corners can't draw a line to any part of the target.
Unit C adds 1 support dice to unit D firing at the Infantry target.
D
support area
C
Area of fire for infantry
support area
support area
E
Artillery unit fires 6 dice and splits its fire as follows:
either: 3 dice at B and 3 dice at C
or: 4 dice at B and 2 dice at C
Infantry unit fires all of its dice against target D.
If target D was out of range, it could fire 1 support dice at target C.
Unit E fires at the infantry, but only fires as if it was a small unit because the target is only within the area of fire of one of its end bases.

Target	Range	Score
In single rank	Long	6+
Unlimbered Artillery		
On soft ground		
Infantry in any formation *	Close	4+
Cavalry charging firers *		
All other targets	Any	5+

* For an assaulting unit to be hit on a 4+ the following conditions apply:
- Cavalry must begin their assault at least partially to the front of the firers.
- Infantry must start their assault within 1 base width of the front of the firers.

Otherwise the chargers are hit on a 5+.

See *Glossary of Terms* for a definition of 'single rank' and 'soft ground'.

The To-hit score on the above table is modified by the 'Points of Advantage' (POA) given in the following table:

POINTS OF ADVANTAGE (POA)	
Target is in March Column or Square, or firers are behind flank or rear, or target is in deep formation at long range	+
Target is in *Skirmisher formation*	–
Skirmishers firing at close range	
Target in cover fired at by:	
Rockets, Howitzers, Mortars, Siege artillery	no POA
All other firing at targets in cover	–
Only artillery can fire at troops 'occupying' buildings	

To count as *firing at the flank or rear* of a unit, the centre of the front edge of the firing unit must be behind a line extending the front edge of the target unit and no part of the firers are directly to the front of any base of the target unit.

When firing, compare the overall POA for dice against each opponent and add them. For example, dice that have 1 plus and 2 minus POA would be on a single net minus (-). No dice may have more than a single net plus (+) or a single net minus (-).

A single net plus (+) makes the To-hit score one less.

A single net minus (-) makes the To-hit score one higher.

The To-hit score may never be higher than 6.

Examples

- Firing at *Skirmishers* (Infantry or Cavalry) at long range the To-hit score is 6.
- Firing at Infantry in single rank at medium range the To-hit score is 5 or higher.
- Firing at the flank of a Cavalry unit at close range the To-hit score is 4 or higher.

Where the To-hit score is different for attachments (for example howitzers firing at buildings), the extra dice provided by the attachment should be rolled separately or should be of a different colour.

Spanish Cazadores officer

RE-ROLLS

The level of training affects a unit's ability to maintain accuracy and rate of fire under battlefield conditions. To reflect this we use the following rule:

- *Veteran* units may choose to re-roll all dice that are 1's.
- *Conscript* and *Irregular* units MUST re-roll all dice that are 6's.
- Dice can only be re-rolled once.

However, attachments to non-*Irregular* units are always considered to be *Drilled*. Therefore, whenever attachments to *Veteran* or *Conscript* units are firing, their dice should be rolled separately or of a different colour. These dice should not be re-rolled. Attachments to *Irregular* units are still treated as *Irregular* and should re-roll dice along with its parent body. If the number of dice rolled is reduced (due to cohesion losses etc.), the owning player can choose which dice to lose.

EFFECT OF HITS FROM FIRING

Each unit rolls the number of dice as calculated above.

After all re-rolls, each dice equal to or above the score required is considered a hit. Add together the hits on a single unit from all sources and consult the results table.

A *Steady* or *Disordered* large unit, or any assaulting *Superior* unit, reduces the number of hits by 1 before consulting the table. However, the number of hits may never be reduced by more than 1. That is, a large *Steady Superior* unit which is assaulting only reduces the hits by 1 (not 2).

RESULTS OF FIRING

Number of hits	Result		Cohesion loss
0	No effect on movement		No effect
1	CMT to Advance	Cavalry must retire to 3MU if closer *	
2			-1 cohesion
3	Retire to 3MU if closer or are *Wavering*, otherwise may not advance.		-1 cohesion
4+	Retire immediately as per *Outcome Moves* table		-2 cohesion *

- A Cavalry unit may choose to stay within 2MU if it has a horse Artillery attachment. If already outside 3MU it may not advance.
- A cavalry unit receiving 4 hits from close range firing during an assault move becomes *Spent*.
- A unit cannot drop 2 cohesion levels unless it received some or all of its fire at close range.
- If none of the firing is at close range a unit that is already *Wavering* does not drop to *Broken*, but instead retires as per the Outcome Moves Table. If any of the firing is at close range a *Wavering* unit will become *Broken*, even if the close range firing does not cause a hit. If the *Wavering* unit is in square it will change to Tactical formation before retiring.

Spanish Cazadore

- A *Guard* unit can never drop by more than 1 cohesion level due to firing in a single phase. It may drop a cohesion level due to firing in both the Assault Phase and the Firing Phase.
- A result of 'may not advance' has no effect on the non-active player.
- A unit forced to retreat to 3MU from the enemy must move the minimum distance to do so. They may make a free wheel forwards or backwards.
- A unit that becomes *Broken* due to fire immediately retreats as per the *Outcome Moves Table*.

Spanish Infantryman

THE COMBAT PHASE

Enemy units in contact fight each other during this phase. See the *Combat Mechanism* section. Each player calculates the number of dice available to each of his units and allocates them against enemy units in contact. He then rolls his dice against each enemy and determines the number of hits on each. After all combat 'hits' have been determined the players then perform actions listed in the *Combat Resolution* table. A second *Combat Phase* may occur if any unit pursues into contact with a different enemy within the first half of its pursuit move.

At the end of any phase in which a Cavalry unit fought a combat, that Cavalry unit automatically becomes *Spent* if it has received a 'hit' from any source during the combat. See the *'Spent Units'* section for more information on when and how Cavalry (and Infantry) become *Spent*.

PROCEDURE

1. Calculate the total number of combat dice available for each unit.
2. Reduce this total due to the affects of cohesion losses.
3. Allocate the remaining dice against available targets.
4. Roll for hits against each unit.
5. Apply result to units and make *Outcome Moves* if required.

THE COMBAT MECHANISM

During the Combat Phase there will be a combat for any non-*Broken* unit which has its front edge in contact with an enemy unit.

Units involved roll the number of dice defined by the *Dice Allowance* table:

Spanish Officer

DICE ALLOWANCE

Unit type	Small Unit	Large Unit
Infantry or Cavalry in Tactical or Extended Line except Irregular light cavalry	6	8
All other troops or situations	4	6

'All other troops and situations' includes all of the following:

- A unit even partially in rough or difficult terrain
- A unit of Infantry in Square
- A unit in March Column formation.
- A unit of Light Infantry entirely in Skirmish formation.
- A unit of *Irregular* light Cavalry in any formation.
- All Units defending or assaulting across an obstacle.
- All Units defending or assaulting buildings.
- A unit of Cavalry fighting Infantry in Square.

DICE ADDITIONS AND LOSSES

<table>
<tr><td colspan="2">Lancers vs Infantry and/or Artillery</td><td rowspan="2">+2 (+1) dice</td><td colspan="2" rowspan="2">* (+1) Units partially lancers or uphill get +1 instead of +2 (Unless lancers are Wavering)</td></tr>
<tr><td colspan="2">Enemy downhill</td></tr>
<tr><td colspan="2">Each supporting unit to flank</td><td>+2 dice</td><td colspan="2">Unless either side is defending an obstacle</td></tr>
<tr><td colspan="2">Unit has rear support</td><td rowspan="2">+1/-1 dice</td><td colspan="2">See Rear Support for details</td></tr>
<tr><td colspan="2">Shock Cavalry vs Infantry or light Cavalry</td><td colspan="2">Unless Infantry is in Square or defending an obstacle</td></tr>
<tr><td colspan="2">Cavalry with artillery attachment</td><td>+1 dice</td><td colspan="2">Only against other Cavalry or Infantry in Square</td></tr>
<tr><td rowspan="2">Cohesion losses:</td><td>Disordered</td><td>Wavering</td><td>Broken</td><td rowspan="2">Infantry and artillery in rain or snow fight as 1 cohesion level lower</td></tr>
<tr><td>Lose 1 dice per 3</td><td>Lose 1 dice per 2</td><td>None</td></tr>
</table>

Units can have a local tactical advantage over their opponents, which can give additional bonus dice as below:

- +2 (+1): The (+1) is used when a unit is only partially lancers or if the unit is only partially uphill. For example, a small unit of light Cavalry could be comprised of 2 bases of hussars and 2 bases of lancers, which would represent 2 under-strength units being grouped together for the duration of the battle. It is also possible for a unit to be uphill with only some of their bases but not others. They will only get the +1 bonus dice in this situation.
- (+1/-1): This unit gets 1 additional dice and removes one dice from each of its opponents.

FLANK SUPPORT

A unit can only gain additional dice for flank support if all of the following apply:

- Infantry and artillery cannot support cavalry.
- The supporting unit is not in combat itself.
- The supporting unit is not *Wavering*.
- The supporting unit is within a base width of the supported unit.
- The enemy is within the Support Area of the supporting unit.

Cavalry to the flank do not provide support dice against enemy Squares or enemy defending an obstacle.

A unit can only gain support dice once on each flank.

The additional dice provided by supporting units are rolled separately and will use the élan re-roll of the supporting unit.

REAR SUPPORT

Rear Support affects the dice allowance for both sides. A unit with rear support receives 1 additional dice, each of its opponents loses 1 dice. For a unit to count as having rear support all of the following must apply:

- Infantry and Artillery can only be supported by other Infantry. The supporting unit must not be in *Skirmish* formation.
- Cavalry can only receive rear support from other Cavalry.
- The supporting unit must be *Steady* or *Disordered*.
- The supporting unit must be capable of reaching the rear of the supported unit in a single move in the terrain crossed and also be within 6MU. Ignore intervening friendly units who are not in contact with the enemy for the purposes of this rule.
- The supporting unit must have 2 bases at least partially behind any base of the supported unit.
- The supported unit must be at least partially forwards of a line extending the supporting unit's front edge.
- A single unit can only provide rear support for a maximum of 2 friendly units, and cannot provide both flank and rear support for the same unit.

Large Infantry and Cavalry units can also support themselves by forming a deeper Tactical formation 3 bases deep. In this formation the unit fires, and fights in combat with the same dice allocation as a small unit. It receives the combat bonus for having rear support regardless of the presence of other units, and it retains the reduction of hits due to it being a large unit.

REAR SUPPORT

Cavalry G is supported by Cavalry H (infantry D does not block the support by Cavalry H).

Infantry A is supported by Infantry D.

Artillery B is not supported (it is not to the front of Infantry D. Cavalry H cannot support Artillery. Infantry E is not directly to it's rear).

Infantry C is not supported (it is not to the front of Infantry F and Infantry E is not directly to its rear.

Infantry D is supported by Infantry E (and not by Cavalry H).

line extending front edge

Infantry F is supported by Infantry E.

INTRODUCTION
TROOP TYPES
GATHERING YOUR FORCES
ORGANISING YOUR ARMY
PLAYING THE GAME
DETAILED RULES
VICTORY AND DEFEAT
SPECIAL FEATURES
REFERENCE SECTION
POINTS SYSTEM
SETTING UP A POINTS BASED GAME
GLOSSARY OF TERMS
USING THESE RULES FOR HISTORICAL BATTLES
USING FIGURES BASED FOR OTHER RULE SETS
DESIGN PHILOSOPHY
APPENDIX 1 – ARMY LISTS
APPENDIX 2 – HISTORICAL BATTLES
ARTWORK REFERENCES
INDEX

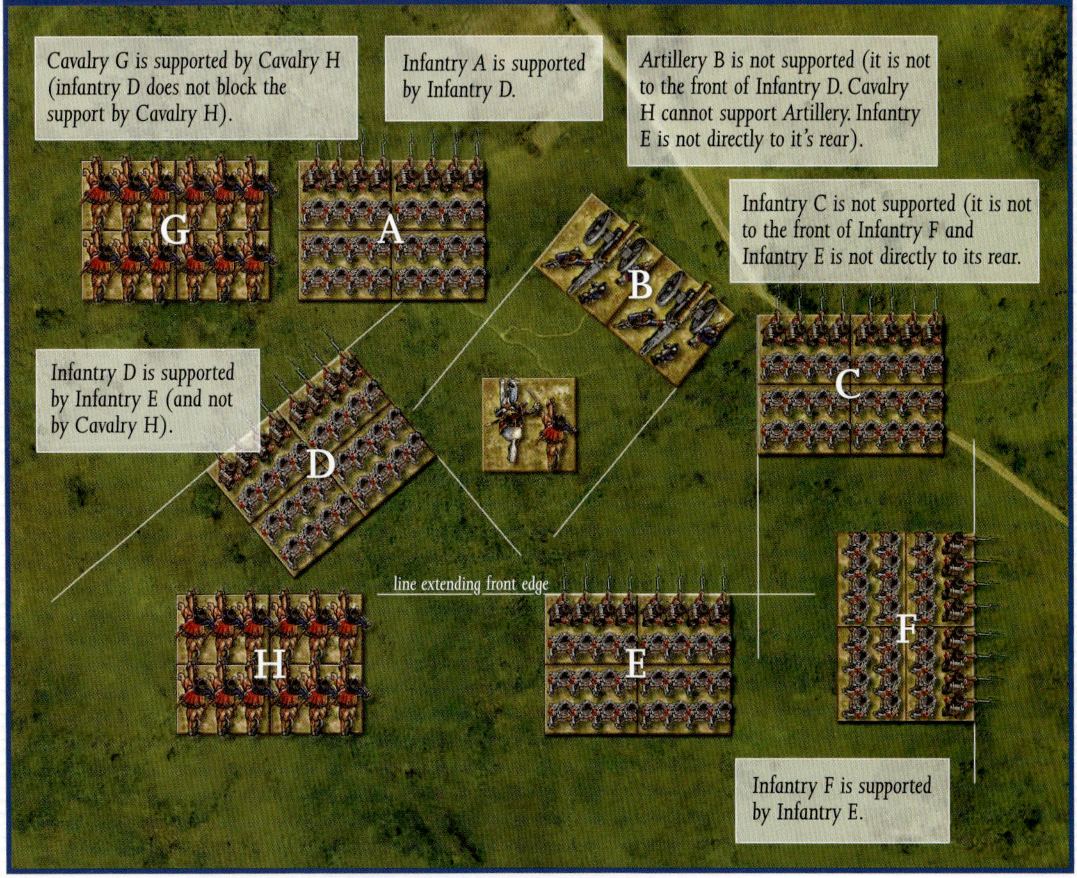

Russian Colour Party

EFFECTS OF COHESION LOSSES ON COMBAT

Infantry and Artillery in snow or rain fight against Cavalry as 1 cohesion level lower. Non- *Skirmishers* in unfavourable terrain fight as 1 cohesion level lower. After all dice allowances have been calculated units with cohesion losses have their number of dice reduced as follows:

- A unit with 1 cohesion loss (or *Steady* and *Spent*) (or *Disordered*) loses 1 dice for each full group of 3 dice.
- A unit with 2 cohesion losses (or *Wavering*) loses 1 dice for each 2 dice.
- A unit with 3 cohesion losses (or *Broken*) does not fight.

Examples

A unit that would normally have 5 dice would lose 1 if *Disordered* and 2 if *Wavering*. A *Wavering* non-Skirmishing unit in rough terrain would lose all of its dice.

DICE ALLOCATION

Each unit now allocates its dice against opponents. In most cases the dice are simply allocated evenly against all opponents however, there will be occasions when this is not the most obvious or optimum method.

Where a unit is in contact with more than 1 opponent use the following rules to allocate dice:

SPLITTING COMBAT BETWEEN MULTIPLE ENEMY UNITS

- Every enemy in contact must be allocated at least 1 dice if 5 or less dice are available and at least 2 dice if 6 or more dice are available. Any remaining dice may be allocated to any target except that the enemy unit nearest the centre of the combat unit's front edge cannot be allocated fewer dice than other enemy units in the combat.
- If there are more enemy units in contact than available dice, the player chooses which unit to allocate dice against, but no unit can be allocated more than 1 dice.

THE TO-HIT VALUE

The score need to hit an opponent with each of your dice is as follows:

THE TO-HIT SCORE		
Normal score required	4+	Modified by the POAs below
Points of Advantage (POA)		
Attacking enemy flank or rear	+/–	Attacker has + POA, defender has – POA
Mounted facing lighter Cavalry	+	Against other mounted only
Mounted fighting Artillery	+	Unless Artillery is defending an obstacle or in cover
Mounted fighting Infantry not in Square	+	Unless infantry are defending an obstacle or in cover
Mounted fighting Infantry in Square	–	Unless Infantry are defending an obstacle (see below)
Fighting across an obstacle	–	Both sides
Infantry facing Shock Cavalry	–	Only in open terrain
March column, *Skirmishers* or Artillery	–	In any terrain

COMBAT DICE ALLOCATION

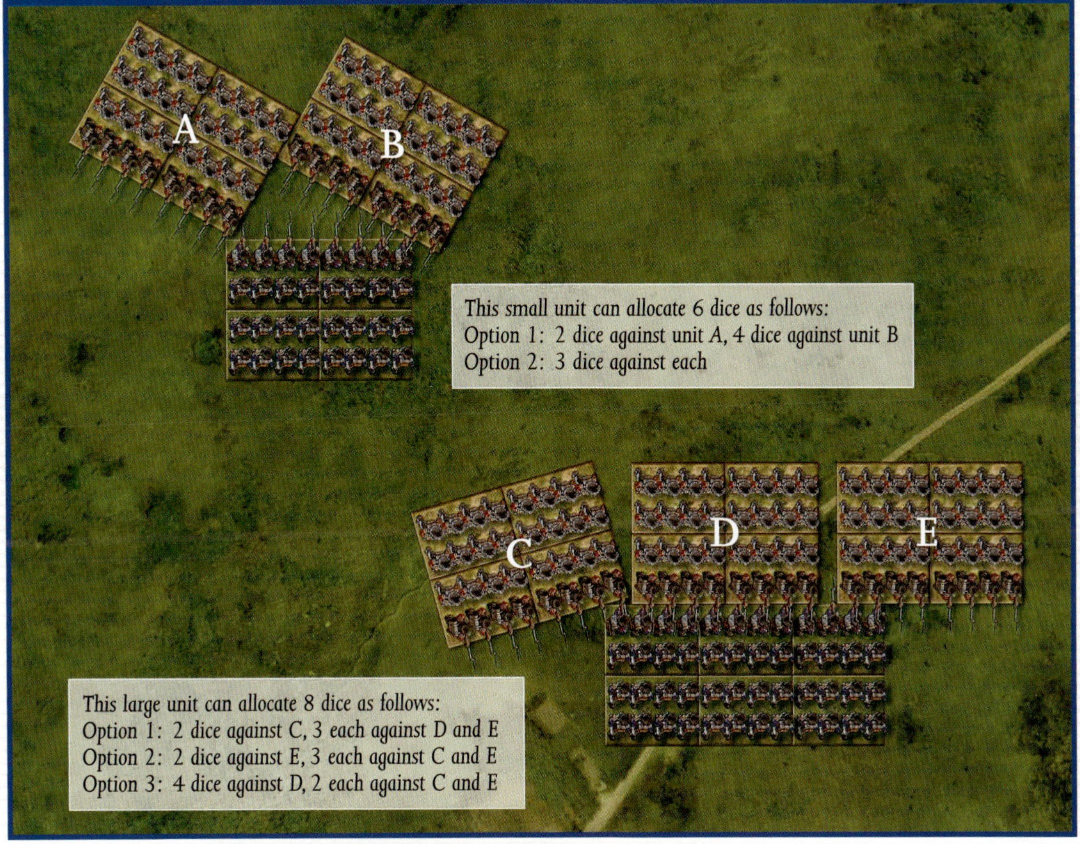

A
B
This small unit can allocate 6 dice as follows:
Option 1: 2 dice against unit A, 4 dice against unit B
Option 2: 3 dice against each
C
D
E
This large unit can allocate 8 dice as follows:
Option 1: 2 dice against C, 3 each against D and E
Option 2: 2 dice against E, 3 each against C and E
Option 3: 4 dice against D, 2 each against C and E

When in close combat, compare the overall POA for dice against each opponent and add them. For example, dice that have 2 plus and one minus POA would be on a net plus one (+). No dice may have more than a double net plus (++) or a double net minus (--).

For different POA, the to hit scores will be as follows:

- ++ POA = 2 or over
- + POA = 3 or over
- No POA = 4 or over
- - POA = 5 or over
- -- POA = 6 or over

A '+' POA for one side does not mean a '-' POA for the other (and visa versa) except for '+/-'.

- All units start with a base To-hit score of 4 or over on each of its dice.
- Cavalry units cannot attack enemy in buildings or across field fortifications.
- Infantry defending an obstacle do not count as 'in Open terrain'

Russian Cossacks

- The 'defending an obstacle' factor counts against both sides, because both sides have a reduced number of men capable of fighting.

LIGHTER CAVALRY

When identifying that Cavalry are 'heavier' or 'lighter' than their opponent's Cavalry the following order is used (from lightest to heaviest):

1. 100% light Cavalry.
2. A unit that is partially light and partially heavy Cavalry.
3. 100% heavy Cavalry. Or a unit of partially light and partially shock heavy Cavalry.
4. A unit that is partially heavy and partially shock heavy Cavalry.
5. 100% shock heavy Cavalry.

Hits against each enemy are added before consulting the *Effect of Combat Hits* table.

ÉLAN RE-ROLLS

The effect of the difference in Élan of the troops is determined by the re-rolling of dice.

- Superior Guard: may re-roll 1s & 2s
- Superior units: may re-roll 1s
- Guard: may re-roll 1s
- Poor troops: MUST re-roll 6s

A commander leading a unit upgrades the Élan of that unit temporarily for combat dice only. This allows the 'To-hit' dice (but not any other type of dice rolls) of that unit to be one re-roll level higher. *Superior Guard* units can elect to re-roll 1s 2s and 3s. *Superior* units and *Guard* units can elect to re-roll 1s and 2s. Average units can elect to re-roll 1s. *Poor* units would not be required to re-roll their 6's. Dice can only be re-rolled once. By leading the unit into combat he is at risk of injury (see *Casualties to commanders*).

Russian Opolchenie Icon Bearer

EFFECT OF COMBAT HITS

Players consult the following table to find what effect the hits received in combat have on their units. A **large unit** has the total hits on it **reduced by one** before consulting this table.

EFFECT OF COMBAT HITS				
Hits received	0-1	2-3	4-5	6+
Cohesion losses	0	1	2	3
Guard only:	0	1	1	2

COMBAT RESOLUTION

The outcome of any combat is determined by the current cohesion state of the player's units. The general rule is that units are retired from combat in order of cohesion state, starting with those that are *Broken* and moving the non-active players unit's first.

To determine the result of close combat, players consult the *Combat Resolution Table*. Note that the outcome result on the non-active player's units may have an effect on the result of the active player's units.

- If both sides' units are *Broken*, the non-active player retires his units first, while the active player's units recover back to *Wavering* if all of their opponents were *Broken*.
- *Disordered* Cavalry in contact with Infantry MAY pass through them. *Steady* Cavalry MUST pass through (see *Pass Through*)
- Infantry do not pursue if defending an obstacle or if they are in Square.
- Artillery never pursue
- Infantry may choose not to pursue if there are un*Broken* enemy Cavalry units within 6MU.
- Troops defending a building from an assault will only retire if *Broken*.
- There is no pursuit against opponents leaving buildings, but assaulting Infantry may occupy them if ALL enemy defenders retire. The assaulting unit immediately enters the buildings in Tactical formation. Initially they are considered to be 'occupying' them and must

COMBAT RESOLUTION

Players perform the following steps in order			
Retire Broken Units			
Non-active player	Retires units in contact and *Broken*	Active player	May pursue * unless *Wavering*.
Recovery	Active players *Broken* units no longer in contact because of enemy retiring are recovered to *Wavering*		
Active player	Retires units in contact and *Broken*	Non-active player	May pursue * unless *Wavering*
Retire Wavering Units			
Non-active player	Retires units in contact and *Wavering*	Active player	May pursue * unless *Wavering*
Active player	Retires units in contact and *Wavering*	Non-active player	May pursue * unless *Wavering*
Retire Disordered Units			
Non-active player	Retires units in contact and *Disordered*	Active player	Halt – No pursuit
Active player	Retires units in contact and *Disordered*	Non-active player	Halt – No pursuit

wait until the next Movement Phase to 'defend' them (see *Special Features / Buildings* and also *Terrain Description, Visibility and Combat Effects / Buildings*). Only 1 Infantry unit may enter a small area of buildings and 2 may enter a large area.

OUTCOME MOVES

At various times during the game a unit may retire without orders from its commander. This will usually be as a result of firing or combat. How a unit moves is determined by their current cohesion level and is given in the *Outcome Moves* table:

OUTCOME MOVES

Unit type	Situation		Cohesion state: Disrupted	Cohesion state: Wavering / Evading	Cohesion state: Broken
Infantry	If facing cavalry and defending obstacle or in square		**Halt**	**Halt**	**Destroyed**
	In the open and in contact with cavalry		Retire D6	Retire D6 +2	
	Otherwise				Retire D6 +4
Cavalry	In contact with enemy		Retire D6 +2	Retire D6 +4	Retire D6 +6
	Otherwise				
Limbered artillery	In contact with enemy		Retire D6	Retire D6 +2	**Destroyed**
	Otherwise				Retire D6 +4
Unlimbered artillery	In contact with enemy cavalry		**Abandoned**	**Destroyed**	**Destroyed**
	In contact with enemy infantry			**Abandoned**	
	Otherwise:	Foot Artillery	Retire D6	Retire D6 +2	Retire D6 +4
		Horse Artillery	Retire D6 +2	Retire D6 +4	Retire D6 +6

Definitions
Halt: The unit remains in place
Retire D6 + X: The unit retires the distance indicated by a roll of a single dice in MU. This may be increased by an additional 'X' number of MU as specified in the table. Unlimbered Artillery end their retire move Limbered.
Destroyed: The unit is immediately destroyed and removed from the table. Other friendly units nearby must take a *Cohesion Test* as if it was *Broken*.
Abandoned: Unlimbered Artillery is abandoned by its gunners (See *The Complex Move Test / Abandoned Guns*).

- The minimum distance for a Retire move is 3MU.
- Any unit retiring from an assault uses the '*Wavering* or *Evading*' column.
- Horse Artillery beginning the move limbered add +2MU to the result.
- Infantry in Square retiring more than 3MU end their move in Tactical formation.
- A retiring unit will halt immediately after crossing an obstacle, or entering an unoccupied building. If the unit is forced to retire into a friendly occupied building, it will treat the entire building as a single friendly unit (see *Bursting Through Friends*).
- The distance measured is halved for any part of the Retire move that passes through difficult terrain.

For Example, if a unit should retire 6MU and Difficult terrain is 4MU away, the moving unit will move 4MU, plus half the remainder of its move, (half of 2MU) for a total of 5MU.

UNITS STILL IN CONTACT

In the rare event that enemy units are still in contact at the end of a Combat Phase (other than as the result of a pursuit) the opposing units are lined up to each other using the following rules:

Single units of the same type (Infantry or Cavalry) that are still in contact are pivoted to directly face each other.

The direction of facing is first determined. The active players unit is wheeled to face this direction, sliding backwards or forwards to maintain contact, while keeping his centre point aligned. The

LINING UP TO A SINGLE ENEMY UNIT

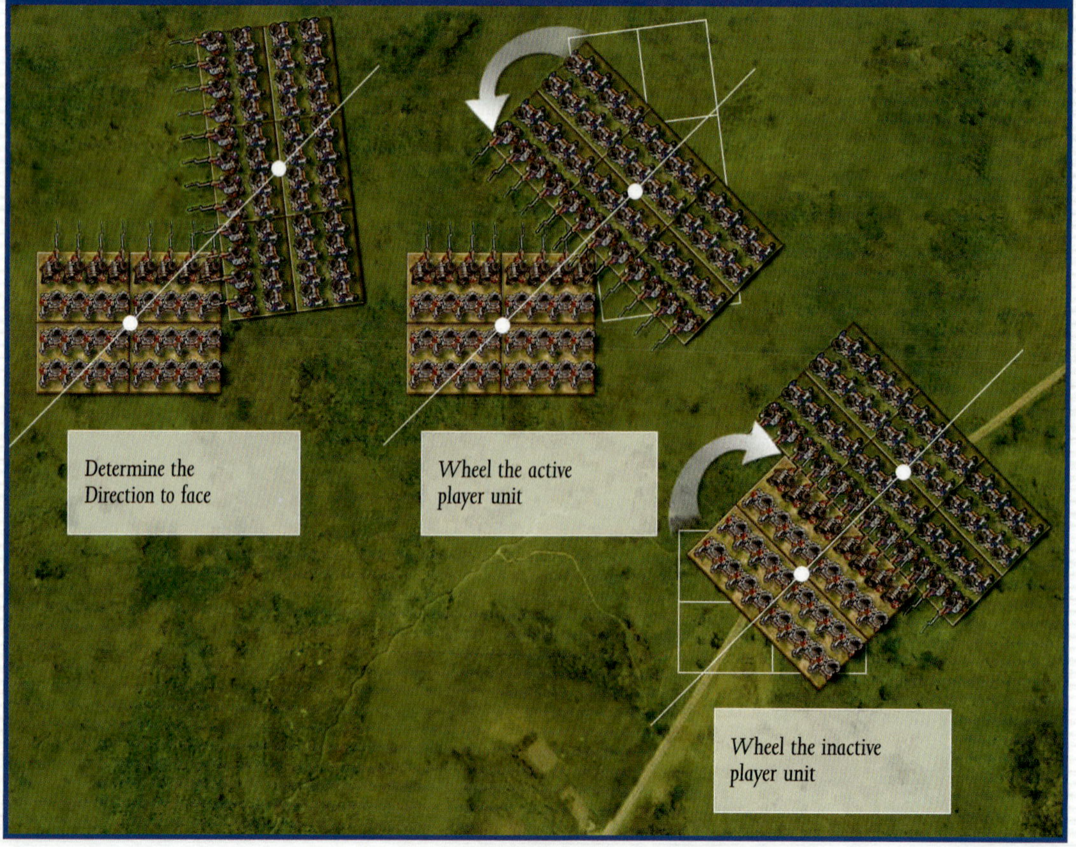

Determine the Direction to face
Wheel the active player unit
Wheel the inactive player unit

LINING UP TO AN ENEMY BATTLE GROUP

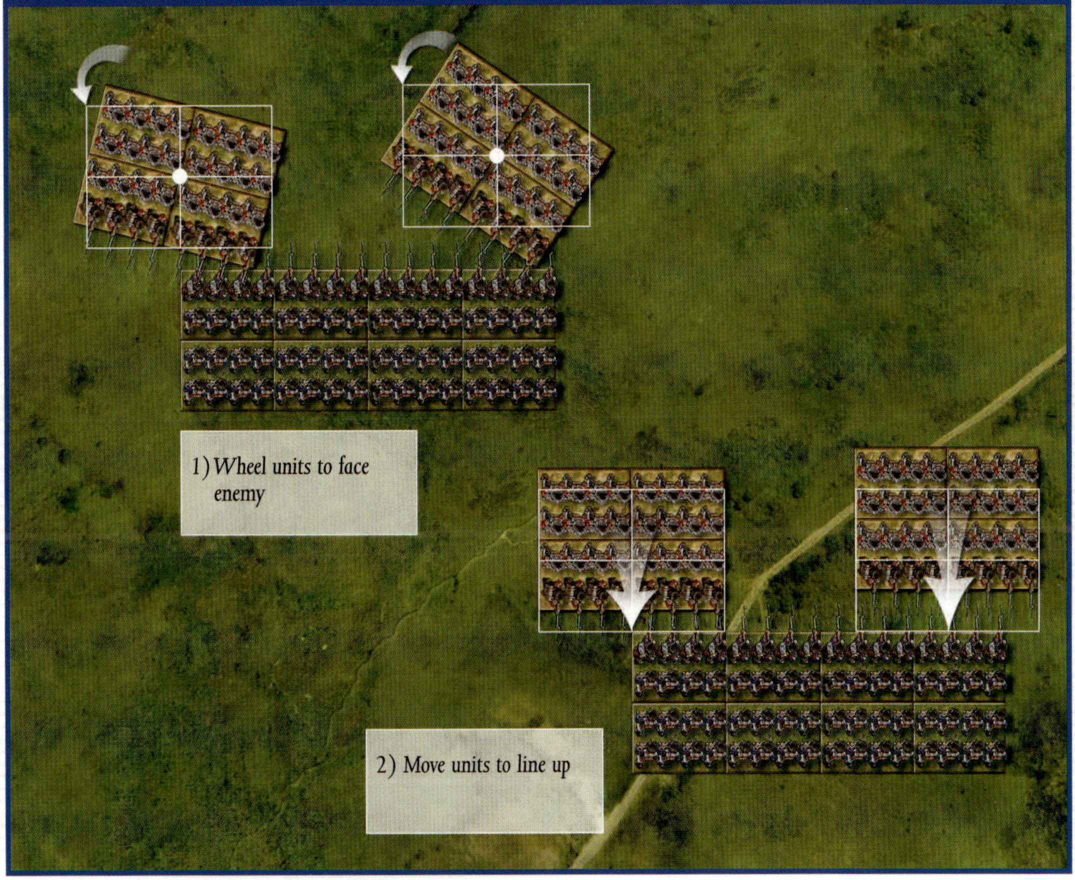
1) Wheel units to face enemy
2) Move units to line up

non-active player does the same until his unit is lined up exactly facing his opponent's unit.

In the following situations the non-active player's unit will not move and only the active player's units will be forced to line up:

- Opposing units are not all of the same type.
- The non-active player's units are forming a *Brigade Group*.
- The non-active player's units are defending an obstacle.

If the active player's units are forced to line up, they are pivoted on their centre point and then slide forwards to re-contact the non-active player's units.

RETIRING UNITS

Units making a retire or an evade move go directly away from the enemy causing them to retreat. If more than one enemy is facing them from different directions, the direction of the retire move should bisect the angle between them. If there are enemy in contact with both flanks, or both their front and rear, the unit will not retire but will take an additional Cohesion loss and stay in place. If the unit becomes *Broken*, or is already *Broken*, then it is *Destroyed*.

A unit that makes an outcome move equal to or greater than its normal move distance in the terrain moved through ends facing the direction of movement (usually away from the enemy). If moving less than its normal move distance it ends facing the direction it came from (facing the enemy). Use the accrual distance moved by the unit, including wheels but not any slides sideways. Actual distance is used because a unit may move extra to pass completely through friends or may be stopped short (as per below).

If there is an obstruction or friendly unit blocking the path of the retire move (other than Infantry entirely in Skirmish order, or any Artillery) then the retiring unit may be able to 'slide' past as follows:

- If an obstruction or friendly unit is less than 4MU behind the retiring unit, the unit may slide up to one base width to avoid it.
- If the obstruction or friendly unit is at least 4MU behind the retiring unit, the unit may slide up to 2 base widths to avoid it.
- The retiring unit may pass through any gap wide enough for a small unit. This will normally be 2 base widths, but may need to be slightly larger if using non-standard bases.
- A large unit in Tactical formation may reduce their frontage by 1 base (into deep formation) to enter the gap. However, no single base may slide more than the 1 or 2 base widths.
- If the *Broken* unit cannot enter the gap in the direction faced, it may pivot one corner backwards by up to 2 MU if this would enable it to enter.
- The length of the retire move is measured in the direction travelled, not the diagonal distance. However, if the unit pivots as above, the pivot is free and any remaining distance is measured in the direction faced after pivoting.
- A unit is only allowed to slide sideways if this would enable it to complete its move without contacting another unit or obstruction.

If the path of a retiring unit is obstructed by friends that cannot be avoided, by sliding sideways and/or pivoting, it will attempt to burst through them.

If the path is obstructed by enemy troops, impassable terrain, the table edge, or by friends it cannot burst through, then the retiring unit will move as far as possible halting 1MU away from the obstruction. Artillery and Infantry entirely in Skirmish order do not count as an obstruction and units may freely pass through them.

BURSTING THROUGH FRIENDS

- A unit attempting to burst through a friendly unit as part of a retire move will pass through such a unit only if it fulfils the requirements described in *Movement Section/Moving through friendly units*. If the retiring unit cannot move through the friendly unit it moves as far as possible, stopping in front of the first unit that it cannot pass through. This unit must take a cohesion test as if it had been passed through.
- A friendly unit passed through by a *Broken* or retiring unit must take a *Cohesion Test*. This is in addition to any tests taken for being within test range of a unit that breaks. If the test is

MOVING *BROKEN* UNITS

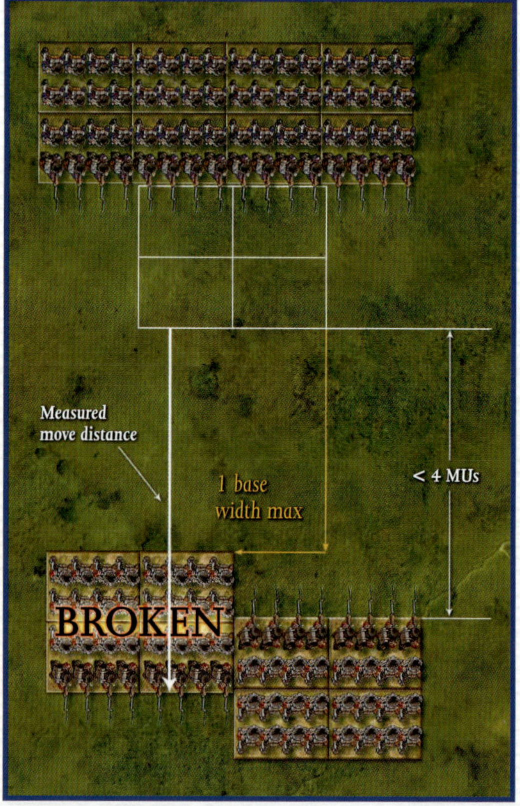

SLIDING AND CONTRACTING A *BROKEN* UNIT

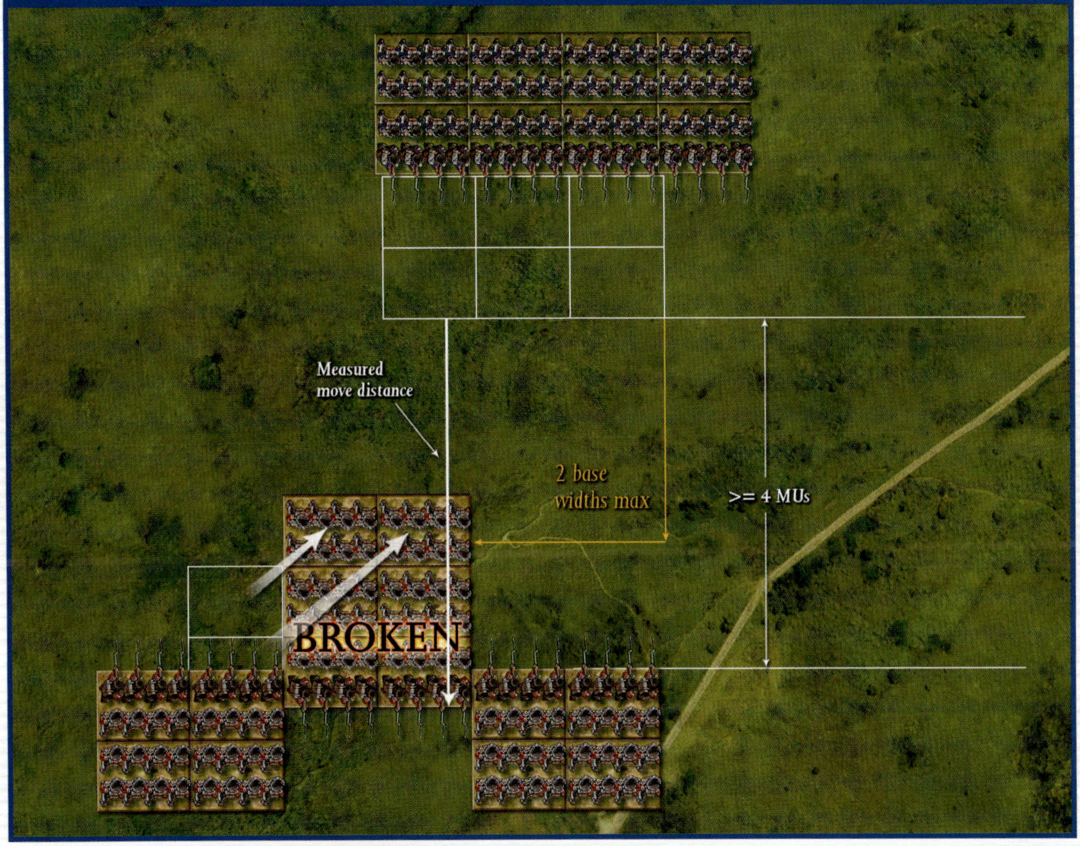

failed only the unit being passed through drops a cohesion level.

TABLE EDGES

- A unit cannot voluntarily leave the table via any edge.
- If a unit reaches a table edge, it must stop. If any move distance remains, then the unit will wheel to line up with that edge. A unit already touching the table edge when it is forced to retire must be removed. Count it as destroyed for victory point purposes.

PURSUIT

At the end of combat a unit may pursue if the *Combat Resolution* table allows.

Pursuit is detailed in the following table:

PURSUIT

Action	Unit/distance	Steady	Disordered
PURSUE	Artillery	Not allowed	
	Infantry D6 MU	Cannot pursue if defending obstacle, or in Square. May always occupy buildings	
		CMT to not pursue	CMT to pursue
	Cavalry D6+2 MU	Must pursue	CMT to not pursue

When pursuing:

- Superior troops MUST re-roll 1's
- Poor Troops MUST re-roll 6's
- If pursuers contact the flank or rear of an enemy unit, the enemy unit will turn to fight but will drop an additional cohesion level.

If the unit becomes *Broken,* or was already *Broken* it is immediately destroyed. If not destroyed, the enemy unit will turn to fight the pursuers, unless still in contact with an opposing unit. If pursuers contact the front edge or corner of a *Wavering* unit it must take a *Cohesion Test* as if being assaulted. For evaluating flank or rear contacts for pursuers (and passing through) the start of the 'assault' move is considered to be their position at the end of combat.

- If enemy are forced to retire from an obstacle, any attacking units allowed to pursue may occupy the position previously held by the defenders, but will not move beyond it.
- Enemy units contacted during the 1st half of a pursuit move cannot make a reaction move, nor may they fire. In addition, another Combat Phase occurs between the contacting units. Only one additional round of combat can take place and all 1st round combats must be completed before any 2nd round combats can occur.
- If a pursuing unit contacts another enemy unit after moving at least half its pursuit move then this combat occurs during the Combat Phase of the next move. In this case the new enemy contacted may make any normal reaction to the assault, but may not fire. However, while the pursuers can't be intercepted, or fired upon they can be attacked while 'in melee' by additional enemy units during the following Assault Phase.

PASS THROUGH

At the end of the combat phase, if *Steady* Cavalry is in contact with only enemy Infantry units the Cavalry MUST pass through them if there is space beyond. *Disordered* Cavalry MAY do so if they pass a CMT (and expend a *Command Point*). The Cavalry are placed with their rear edge touching the enemy far edge (or corner) before making their 'pass through' move. If there is insufficient space the Cavalry must retire instead. The distance moved is always D6+2 MU directly ahead and is treated as a pursuit move in all other respects.

CASUALTIES TO COMMANDERS

During the Napoleonic wars commanders often led their troops into battle. Because of this commanders often became casualties during the fighting.

To represent this, a player rolls on the 'Casualties to Commanders' table whenever the following occurs:

Whenever a unit led by a commander takes 3 or more hits in a single firing or Combat Phase, the player causing the hits tests immediately to see if he has injured the commander. Test immediately after firing or combat has been adjudicated, but before any test for seeing *Broken* units.

Polish Officer

It is possible for a unit to fight 2 rounds of combat in a single phase due to the effect of pursuing units. These 2 combats count as separate phases for counting the hits required. Hits normally ignored by *Superior* or large units still count towards the 3 hits required to cause a casualty to a commander.

PROCEDURE

Roll a number of dice per commander as given on the chart below. If ALL of the dice rolled are equal to or higher than the number required, then the commander has become a casualty.

The 'Rifles' column is used if there are any riflemen (including attachments) in any of the units causing casualties on the commander's unit.

It can be seen that an attached *Brigade Commander* is quite easy to hit, while a *Corps*

CASUALTIES TO COMMANDERS

A player rolls to injure a commander if he causes **3** hits in a single phase on his unit

Commander type	Number of dice to roll	Hits from Shooting		Hits from Combat	
		Rifles	Muskets or Artillery	Enemy retires	any other result
Corps Commander	3				
Division Commander	2	5+	6+	5+	6+
Brigade Commander	1				

Commander is very difficult to hit. This is deliberate and is done to reflect the high number of lower level commanders that became casualties during many battles of the period.

EFFECTS

If a *Corps Commander* or a *Division Commander* becomes a casualty, the owner loses that commander's abilities until the end of his next Recovery Phase, at which time a replacement is available. A *Corps Commander* is always replaced with one of his *Division Commanders*. If the *Division Commander* was an *Exceptional Commander*, then the replacement *Corps Commander* is a *Skilled Commander*. In all other case he is replaced with a *Competent Commander*. If the *Division Commander* was 'charismatic' he would remain so after his promotion to *Corps Commander*.

If the *Division Commander* has any unit within his command that has an attached *Brigade Commander*, he may sacrifice him to replace his *Division Commander* at the beginning of his next Recovery Phase rather than at the end. Simply remove the *Brigade Commander* and replace it with a normal base. The replacement *Division Commander* is always *Competent* and is placed with the unit whose *Brigade Commander* was removed. He may move freely at the start of the Recovery Phase. If a *Brigade Commander* becomes a casualty, there is no effect other than the permanent loss of this attachment – replace it with a normal base.

Polish Light Infantryman

THE RECOVERY PHASE

In this phase the active player can reorganise or rally his units. Any unit may attempt to recover its cohesion, even if the cohesion loss occurred earlier in the current player turn.

- The non-active player may first move any of his commanders up to 4MU in preparation for his next turn.
- The active player may then move any of his commanders up to 4MU.

The active player may then take a *Cohesion Test* to recover his units.

Tests have the following restrictions:

- A *Brigade Commander* can only recover the unit he is attached to.
- A *Corps* or *Division Commander* can only recover a unit of his own command which is within 4MU.
- Each *Commander* may only try to recover one unit per Recovery Phase.
- The active player returns his *Command Point* markers (ADCs) to their respective commanders.

- A unit passing a recovery test may recover facing any direction.
- A *Broken* unit always rallies into Tactical formation (limbered if Artillery).
- *A Broken* unit MUST attempt to rally in the owning player's first Recovery Phase after it has been *Broken*. If the attempt fails, the unit is permanently removed from the table.

THE MORALE AND RECOVERY MECHANISM

This section contains the mechanisms to determine what your troops do in various battlefield situations.

COHESION

A Unit has 4 possible levels of cohesion:

- Steady: No cohesion losses
- Disordered: 1 cohesion loss
- Wavering: 2 cohesion losses
- Broken: 3 cohesion losses

Abandoned Artillery only may accumulate 3 cohesion losses without being *Broken* (although they count as lost for victory point purposes).

Each time a unit has a reason to drop a cohesion state it moves its state to the next lower one. For example, a single drop from *Steady* would be to *Disordered*. A double drop would be to *Wavering*. Units may temporarily lose cohesion levels due to other factors (weather, terrain etc). These will cause the unit to fire and fight as if they were at a lower cohesion level (even *Broken*), but in all other respects these are ignored.

Cohesion states can be indicated by positioning the bases of a unit as a visual reminder, or you may prefer to use counters. These alternative methods are shown below. In all cases - when a unit is *Broken*, its bases are turned around and it will then flee at the time specified in the turn sequence.

MARKING UNIT COHESION LOSSES

SPENT UNITS

An Infantry or Cavalry unit can also have a permanent state of *Spent*. This occurs for any Infantry or Cavalry unit that has rallied after being *Broken*. A cavalry unit only may will also become *Spent* if it takes 4 hits from shooting, or at the end of a combat phase in which it takes at least one hit. This may occur at the end of either of the 2 possible Combat Phases with large units counting all hits for the purposes of this rule. Artillery units can never become *Spent*.

Being *Spent* has the following effects:

- A *Spent*, but otherwise *Steady*, unit fires and fights as if 1 cohesion level lower. There is no additional effect on a *Disordered* or *Wavering* unit.
- *Spent* Cavalry are no longer impetuous (if relevant).
- A *Spent* Infantry unit may never form Extended Line.
- A *Spent* Infantry unit that breaks a 2nd time will be destroyed and is removed at the end of its outcome move.
- A *Spent* unit requires the expenditure of a *Command Point* to declare an assault or an intercept move unless they are *shock* or *Guard* Cavalry or are *Guard* Infantry.
- To signify that the unit is *Spent* a base is permanently removed from it. The missing base will always be from the back rank if the unit is in a formation of more than a single base deep. Since all units start the battle with an even number of bases a *Spent* marker is not required. A *Spent* unit in Tactical, Square or 2 deep Skirmish formation still takes up the same physical space that it would if the base not been removed. Players should not overlap this space with other units. All distances are measured as if the base had not been removed. In some circumstance it may be useful to replace the *Spent* base with a blank base of the same size.

HALTED

One additional condition may require a temporary marker. This is the 'no advance' state as a result of firing. This only lasts for the duration of the Movement Phase following so is not difficult to remember. As an aid to this it is suggested that a single base of the affected unit be temporarily turned 90 degrees for the duration of that Movement Phase.

COHESION TESTS

Tests are carried out in the circumstances given in the following tables:

During the Assault Phase only:

<table>
<tr><th colspan="4">RESPONDING TO AN ASSAULT</th></tr>
<tr><th colspan="2">Attempted activity</th><th>Score required</th><th>Result if test failed</th></tr>
<tr><td rowspan="3">Infantry assaulted by Cavalry in the open & not in Square</td><td>Form Square from Extended Line</td><td>6+</td><td rowspan="3">Cohesion Loss</td></tr>
<tr><td>Form Square from Tactical or March Column</td><td rowspan="2">5+</td></tr>
<tr><td>Stand and fire</td></tr>
<tr><td colspan="4">Note: Infantry not in square take an additional automatic cohesion loss if assaulted by cavalry starting from within 2MU</td></tr>
<tr><td colspan="2">Any friendly unit burst through by impetuous troops</td><td rowspan="4">5+</td><td rowspan="3">Cohesion Loss</td></tr>
<tr><td colspan="2">Infantry in Square assaulted by other Infantry</td></tr>
<tr><td colspan="2">A Wavering unit having an assault declared on it</td></tr>
<tr><td colspan="2">Light Cavalry Skirmishers choosing to counter-charge non-Skirmisher cavalry</td><td>Evade</td></tr>
<tr><td colspan="2">Artillery choosing to stand and fire</td><td>4+</td><td>Abandon Guns</td></tr>
</table>

These tests are described in more detail in the *Assault Phase* section.

During the Recovery Phase only:

RECOVERY TESTS				
Attempted Activity			Score Required	Result if test failed
Rallying a *Broken* unit		1 attempt only	6+	Unit Destroyed
Recovering abandoned Artillery *	3 cohesion losses			
	1 or 2 cohesion losses		5+	
Recovering cohesion losses for any unit				No Effect
* See *Abandoned Guns* for more details				

At any time as a reaction to battlefield events:

OTHER COHESION TESTS		
Attempted Activity	Score Required	Result if test failed
Whenever *Broken* non-*Skirmishing* Infantry first passes within 4MU	5+	Cohesion Loss
If within 4MU of non-*Skirmishing* Cavalry at the time they break		
If 'burst through' by friends as part of an outcome move		
When a *Commander* or officer attachment with the unit becomes a casualty		

- Infantry in Skirmish formation do not cause other units to test if they are *Broken*.
- *Guard* units do not test for seeing broken non-*Guard* units
- Artillery that have been *Broken* do not cause other units to test.
- Tests for *Broken* Cavalry and for casualties to commanders are taken at the end of the phase, but before any outcome move is made.
- Tests for *Broken* Infantry passing within 4MU or for units bursting through are taken at the end of each *Broken* units move.

French Cohesion Markers

PROCEDURE

Each time one of his units is required to test for any of the above reasons, the player rolls the number of dice as follows:

- Veterans: 3 dice
- Drilled & Irregulars: 2 dice
- Conscripts: 1 die

Charismatic commander with unit	+1 dice	Does not affect Artillery
Conscripts		If in a defensive position, or if having rear support
Troops in Extended Line:	-1 dice	if not defending obstacle, or hill/slope

- Cavalry and Infantry (not Artillery) led by a charismatic commander gain an additional dice.
- *Conscripts* gain an additional dice if they have another unit giving them rear support, or are in a Defensive Position.
- *Conscripts* in Extended Line automatically fail a test they are forced to take unless they have another unit supporting them or are defending a hill or are behind an obstacle.

- Units in Extended Line and not in a Defensive Position have their dice reduced by one.
- To pass the test any ONE of the dice rolled must be greater than or equal to the score given in the tables above.

ÉLAN RE-ROLLS

The effect of the difference in Élan of troop types is determined by the re-rolling of dice. Units may (or must) re-roll some of their dice depending on the result and their Élan:

- Superior Guard: may re-roll all 1's and 2's if they fail their test.
- Superior troops: may re-roll all 1's if they fail their test.
- Guard: may re-roll all 1's if they fail their test.
- Poor troops: must re-roll all 6's if they pass their test.

Tests triggered by firing and combat are taken after all firing and fighting has been completed in the phase, except that 1st and 2nd rounds of combat are treated separately. All other tests are taken immediately at the time of occurrence.

Each unit is tested independently in the order chosen by the owning player. A failed test may result in a unit becoming *Broken*, which in turn may trigger additional tests. A unit may be required to take a second test if other units close by fail their own test. For example: 2 units are within 4MU of a unit that becomes *Broken* this phase. The first unit to test successfully passes, but the 2nd unit fails and in doing so becomes *Broken*. This causes the 1st unit to take another test. A failed *Cohesion Test* will usually result in the unit dropping a single cohesion level. The only exceptions to this are:

- *Skirmishers* trying to stand when assaulted by non-Skirmishers: A failure results in the *Skirmishers* being forced to evade.
- Artillery attempting to stand and fire when assaulted: A failure results in the Artillery being abandoned.

When a unit is testing to recover its cohesion in the recovery phase a failed result in has no effect. A successful recovery test will result in a unit gaining one level of cohesion.

i.e. From *Disordered* to *Steady*
From *Wavering* to *Disordered*
From *Broken* to *Wavering*

A *Commander* can only recover one unit, which may be any unit of the corps for a *Corps Commander*, of his own division for a *Division Commander*, or his parent unit for a *Brigade Commander*. A commander leading a unit in contact with enemy cannot make a recovery test.

BROKEN UNITS

Broken units that have not already moved this turn make an additional move during their own Movement Phase. They move a normal move distance with the following criteria.

1. They must end their move further away from all enemy than when they started.
2. They must end their move nearer their own base edge, or the edge of the table that they arrived on if flank marching. They must end their move as close as possible to that edge after complying with rule 1 above.
3. All *Broken* units end their move facing the direction of movement.
4. They may not pass through another unit other than Artillery or Infantry *Skirmishers*.
5. If the Broken unit cannot complete its move, it will move as far as possible and then halt.

Additionally:

- *Broken* units lose all attachments other than *Skirmishers*. Remove these attached bases and replace them with 'normal' bases matching the rest of the unit.
- A *Broken* unit may not declare an assault, counter-charge or fire.
- *Broken* units must attempt to rally during the first Recovery Phase after it becomes *Broken*.

If the *Broken* unit either fails to rally or doesn't attempt to rally then it is destroyed and removed from the table.

- All *Broken* units count as lost for victory point purposes.
- All *Broken* units that rally lose a single base permanently. This is to signify that the unit is now *Spent*. A base is not removed from Cavalry units which have already lost such a base for being *Spent*. A unit can only ever lose a single base for being *Spent*.
- *Broken* Infantry units that are already *Spent* cannot rally and are removed from play at the beginning of the Recovery Phase. This means that an Infantry unit can only ever be rallied once.
- If a *Broken* unit is contacted by an enemy assault or pursuit they are immediately destroyed and are removed from the table. Any *Division Commander* or *Corps Commander* with the unit may become a casualty.

British Infantryman

LINE OF COMMUNICATIONS

The Line of Communications (LOC) is represented by the LOC marker touching a player's base edge. Units of both sides may pass though LOC*s* as if passing through other friendly units of their own command except that the LOC cannot move under any circumstances. If the LOC has a friendly unit in contact with it, the enemy may not move into contact with it unless it makes an assault move, which may be into contact with either the unit or the LOC. If both players have units in contact with the LOC, they will fight as if in frontal contact with each other in their current formation.

If at any time an enemy unit is in contact with a player's LOC it is considered to be *occupied* if:

- The occupying unit is not *Wavering* or *Broken*
- The occupying unit is not in contact with one of the player's own units (either directly or by both players being in contact with the LOC)
- The occupying unit is not Artillery.
- The occupying unit is not in March Column.

If a player's LOC is *occupied* the following rule is in effect:

- ALL *Cohesion Tests* have 1 added to the required results dice roll. Note that tests requiring a 6 to pass will automatically fail and that *Broken* units cannot recover. *Broken* units will automatically be removed during the Recovery Phase as long as their LOC is occupied.

VICTORY AND DEFEAT

T*here are different ways* to identify the victor in a game:

If refighting a historical battle or scenario, the winning conditions should be defined beforehand, based upon the historical outcome of the battle.

If using a 'what-if' scenario, then the game designer will also have to specify what the exact objectives are for each side and what the victory conditions are.

For a one-off or points-based game the following rules may be used:

At the start of the game calculate your army's combat value as follows:

- Each small unit: 2 points
- Each large unit: 3 points

Add the total points for each army's units to give each player their Army Combat Value (ACV)

During the game each army loses attrition points as follows:

Each unit *Broken*, destroyed, abandoned or having left the table:

- Small unit: 2 points
- Large unit: 3 points

Spent units (unbroken and still on-table):

- Each base removed from a small Cavalry unit: 1/2 point
- Each base removed from any other unit: 1 point

There are 2 ways of winning a points based Game:

1. An army is considered to be defeated if at the start of the Recovery Phase it has accumulated attrition points equal to or greater than half of its ACV. Unless both sides suffer a simultaneous defeat, (which is a draw), their opponent has achieved a **Victory**.

French Grenadier

2. An army is considered to be defeated if it has received so many more casualties than its opponent, that their commander deems it not worth continuing the fight.

To identify the point at which this occurs we use the following rule:

At the start of the Recovery Phase, if one side has lost at least **30%** of its ACV in attrition points and his opponent has lost less than **10%** of his own attrition points then his opponent has gained a **Victory.**

At the start of the Recovery Phase, if one side has lost at least **40%** of its ACV in attrition points and his opponent has lost less than **20%** of his own attrition points then his opponent has gained a **Victory.**

In stand-alone games the game is now over. In campaign or scenario games, additional rules may be provided to cover a retreat from the battlefield.

If playing to a time limit and neither army is defeated at the pre-set time limit:

- A side that inflicted at least 12 more attrition points than the enemy and >= 3:1 gains a **Major Victory.**
- Failing that, a side that inflicted at least 8 more attrition points than the enemy and >= 2:1 gains a **Moderate Victory.**
- Failing that, a side that inflicted at least 4 more attrition points than the enemy gains a **Marginal Victory.**
- If none of the above apply, the game is a draw.

Note that there is no recovery phase for the last move of a game in which neither army is defeated.

BONUS POINTS

A victory is upgraded or downgraded by one level if one side has at least 2 more units of fresh Cavalry than his opponent.

SPECIAL FEATURES

BUILDINGS

Buildings are a special feature that has restrictions both on troops attacking and defending them. The area defined as 'buildings' may represent groups of buildings or a single large structure.

To enter buildings all units must pass a CMT unless they are in March Column and moving along a road.

Units within buildings may be in one of 3 formations:

- In March Column– only if moving on a road.
- In Tactical formation – available to Infantry only. They are considered to be 'occupying' the buildings
- Defending – available to Infantry units only. They should be placed around the perimeter of the building area

Artillery and Cavalry may only move though buildings if they are in March Column and moving along a road. All units in March Column in a building are also considered to be 'occupying' it.

Infantry units may 'occupy' buildings, treating them as rough terrain. Infantry in Extended Line or Skirmish formation will change to Tactical on entering the buildings. Figures occupying buildings should be placed inside the building area in Tactical formation. If the figures cannot be placed in the

UNITS IN BUILDINGS

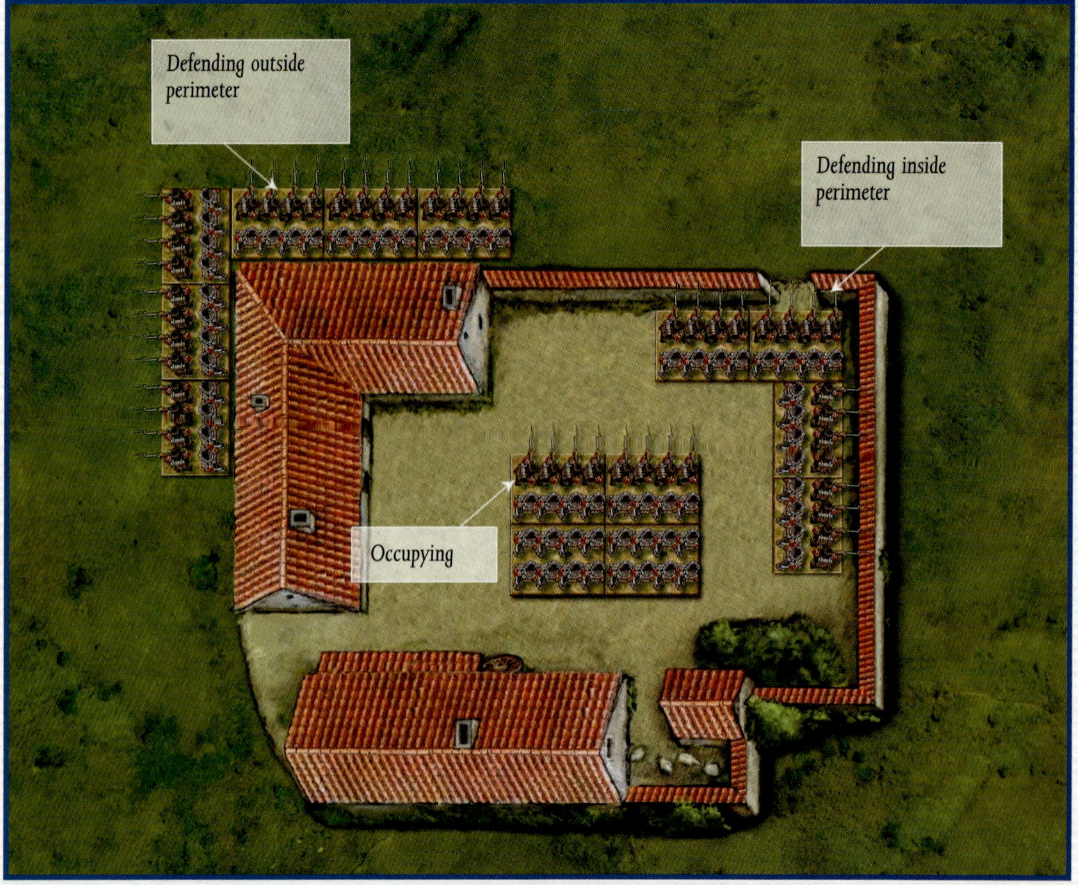

building, split the front and back rank bases to either side of the building, with all bases facing in the same direction.

Infantry may also choose to 'defend' the buildings. They can do this immediately on passing a CMT to enter, or they may change from passing through or March Column to 'defending' without a CMT, taking their full movement allowance to do so. To show that a unit is defending buildings its bases should be placed in single rank around the perimeter.

Infantry defending buildings must be placed with either their front or their rear edge touching the perimeter of the buildings. All measurements to and from units in a building is taken to or from the nearest point of the perimeter of the building. The actual position of the units within the building is ignored for all purposes. The building is considered to be defended, occupied or empty.

Infantry moving (or pursuing) into buildings after all of their close combat opponents retire are initially considered to be 'occupying' and must wait until their next Movement Phase if they wish to change their status to 'defending'.

When occupying buildings units are considered to be:

- In rough terrain for cohesion purposes.
- In cover when fired at (by artillery only).
- In cover but not defending an obstacle when in combat.

Infantry defending buildings are considered to be:

In open terrain for cohesion purposes.
In cover when fired at.
Defending an obstacle when in combat

Limbered Artillery and units in March Column may only leave a building along a road. Units in March Column or 'occupying' may leave without passing a CMT. Infantry defending buildings must pass a CMT to leave or to change to 'occupying' or to column. Units not in column may leave in any direction taking a full single move. After leaving they should be placed in Tactical formation with as much as possible of their rear edge touching the building. If there is no space to place them, they cannot leave the building in that direction.

A unit may move directly from one building to another by passing a CMT if the gap between the 2 buildings is 2MU or less. It may end its move either occupying or defending the building moved to.

A building can only contain 1 unit. There is no flank or rear for troops in a building regardless of formation.

GENERAL RULES FOR COMBAT AGAINST DEFENDED BUILDINGS

- Only Infantry can assault defended buildings.
- Each assaulting Infantry unit receives defensive fire at close range from defending enemy Infantry.
- Each unit in combat against buildings receives an allocation of 4 dice (counting as small and 'other troops or situations'). A unit defending buildings receives an allocation of 4 dice against each attacking enemy unit. There is no benefit for a 'large' Infantry unit other than the reduction of hits by 1.
- Infantry defending a building gain rear support if the supporting unit is Infantry outside the buildings, with at least part of the building area directly to their front. The supporting Infantry must be capable of moving into contact with the building by a single move. This move cannot cross, within 4MU, the front face of an enemy unit. If the unit in a building qualifies for rear support, each of the enemy units in combat with it lose 1 dice, and the defending unit gains 1 dice.
- All other factors that may change the number of dice rolled are ignored, other than the normal reductions for cohesion losses.
- Both sides will be on –POA.
- Units defending a building will only leave it from an outcome move if they are *Broken.*

FIRING TO OR FROM BUILDINGS

- Only artillery units may fire at a unit occupying a building, both infantry and artillery may fire at a unit defending a building.
- All units firing into buildings at close or medium range receive 4 dice.
- Artillery other than attachments cannot fire from a building.
- Infantry defending a building fire at close or medium range with 4 dice against each unit capable of firing at them this phase, or (as defensive fire) against enemy assaulting them. If no enemy unit is capable of firing at them, they may fire with 4 dice at the closest single enemy unit within their normal range. Note that this means that unreformed Infantry can return fire at targets at 6MU, but may only fire at a target not firing at them within 2MU.
- Artillery attachments provide additional dice for both sides against one target only.
- Artillery firing at long range at units in a building receives its normal allocation of dice.
- Weather effects are ignored for Infantry defending buildings.
- Both sides will hit on a 5 at close range and a 6 at medium or long range, except that dice provided by rocket and howitzer attachments and for mortar and siege Artillery units will hit on 5 at all available ranges.
- Units may not fire into or from buildings if any of the occupants are in contact with an enemy.

French Middle Guard Drummer

FIELD FORTIFICATIONS

Field Fortifications (earthworks, redoubts, etc) are considered to be a defensive *obstacle* and *cover*. A small fortification cannot measure more than 4MU in any direction and a large one more than 6MU. Only Infantry and Artillery may defend a fortification, although cavalry may freely enter from the rear unless it is already occupied by another friendly unit. A small fortification can only be defended by small units, and a large one by either small or large units. No more than 3 artillery bases may ever be placed in a fortification of any size. Larger fortifications may be placed if playing a historical game or a special scenario. One side of the fortification should be designated the 'rear' and is considered to be 'open'. Firing by infantry into or from fortifications is treated the same as firing into or from buildings.

Artillery firing from a fortification can choose the following dice allocation:

- Fire with normal number of dice at a single target.
- Fire with 2/3 dice at each of 2 targets (round to nearest whole number).
- Fire with half dice at each of 3 targets.

For example, a small unit of heavy artillery may fire 4 dice at a single target, 3 dice at each of 2 targets, and 2 dice at each of 3 targets. Normal POAs apply for all artillery fire. Firing from fortifications by both infantry and artillery is affected by rain or snow.

Units may not fire out of the rear of fortifications. Units firing into the rear of a fortification gain the +POA for *Firing at a Flank or Rear* and the defenders are considered to be in the open.

Assaulting the front or sides of a field fortification is treated as if assaulting troops who are defending buildings, except that the defenders also count as being uphill. Assaulting the rear of the fortification always counts as *Assaulting a Flank or Rear* (regardless of the defenders facing), and the defenders are considered to be in the open. Units assaulting the rear must be able to contact it with their own front edge or front corner. A unit in a fortification may receive rear support, counting the rear of the fortification as the unit's own rear.

RIVERS AND STREAMS

Rivers and streams are treated identically, except that a river must be at least 2MU wide and a stream must be less than 2MU wide. A stream is likely to be shallower than a river.

Crossing a river or stream is treated as crossing an obstacle for movement unless it is ankle deep, in which case it is ignored, or it is dried up.

Infantry and Artillery can defend the banks of rivers and streams counting as *defending an obstacle*. To do so the unit must be facing the river, with the centre of its front edge or with both front corners, within 2MU of it. Defending a river has no effect on firing. Cavalry cannot assault across a defended river unless it is ankle deep or has dried up.

A dried-up river is counted as a gulley for its entire length. A dried up stream is ignored for all purposes. Infantry and artillery defending the bank of a dried up river count as being uphill if they are outside and are being assaulted by units at least partially inside. The defenders count as being in the open if assaulted by cavalry, but do not have to take a CT to stand and fire – they must still take a test if they wish to form square.

A unit assaulting across a river may fight in combat as if it had additional cohesion losses.

River Height	Effect on Defenders	Effect on Attackers
Water is shoulder high	Defenders are *defending an obstacle*	Attacker fights as if 2 levels of cohesion lower
Water is waist high	Defenders are *defending an obstacle*	Attacker fights as if 1 level of cohesion lower
Water is ankle deep	Defenders are *defending an obstacle*	No additional effect
River has dried up	Defenders fight as if uphill in the open	Attacker fights as if in rough
Stream has dried up	No effect	No effect

BRIDGES AND FORDS

Units crossing a bridge or ford must pass a CMT as if crossing an obstacle, unless they are in March Column, or if the river is ankle deep or has dried up. Crossing a river by bridge is otherwise treated as crossing an obstacle.

A unit of Infantry or Cavalry may assault across a bridge of a ford:

- If the assaulting unit is in March Column the defenders count as *defending an obstacle*. The assaulting unit also has the normal reductions for being in March Column.
- If the assaulting unit is in Tactical formation the defenders count as *defending an obstacle*. If the Water is shoulder high the assaulting unit also fights at 1 cohesion level lower.
- Units cannot assault across a defended bridge in any other formation.
- Any unit may choose to assault across the river instead of the bridge. This may be preferable in some cases, particularly if the river is less than waist high.

OBSTACLES

These can be any linear position that cannot simply be ignored. Walls and hedges around otherwise open or rough fields are typical examples used in the game, as are streams and rivers. For historical battles other types may be considered, such as a sunken road or a steep ridge.

In most cases *obstacles* can only be crossed with a CMT. To cross an *obstacle* a unit must start with any part of its front edge, or front corner, touching the *obstacle* and parallel to it. If the *obstacle* has no straight edge, the unit crossing must have either the centre of its front edge in contact with it, or its 2 front corners. After crossing, the unit should be placed a minimum distance forwards, and parallel to its original position with its rear edge or a rear corner touching the *obstacle*.

Units defending walls count as behind cover if fired at from the front only. No other *obstacles* give the benefit of cover. However, if both players agree before the game, other types of *obstacles* may be counted as cover if there is reasonable justification.

When assaulting an *obstacle* the following rules are in effect:

- Cavalry gain no benefit from defending an *obstacle*.
- Both sides have a –POA for fighting across *an obstacle*.
- Mounted do not gain a +POA for fighting Infantry that are not in *Square*.
- Mounted do not receive the –POA if the Infantry are in *Square*
- Infantry do not receive the –POA for facing *Shock* Cava*lry*.
- Defending Infantry will not retire unless they become *Broken*.
- Defenders do not pursue defeated enemy.

REFERENCE SECTION

GROUND SCALE

For the purposes of these rules we use a standard ground scale of 1MU = 67 yards (60 meters). Because we use a different MU size for the various figure sizes this gives us the following:

- 20–28mm figures: ground scale 1:1600 or 1 inch (25mm) = 50 yards (40m)
- 12–18mm figures: ground scale 1:2400 or 1 inch (25mm) = 67 yards (60m)
- 5–10mm figures: ground scale 1:3200 or 1 inch (25mm) =100 yards (80m)

10mm figures use either the 5–10mm or the 12–18mm figure scales according to taste and basing requirements.

TIME SCALE

A normal pair of game turns in the rules represents all the activities and movements taking place within a 20min period.

FIGURE SCALE

Each base in the game represents an area covered by a number of men in formation, along with their equipment. This can vary due to organisation and casualties, but is always within a fixed range. This is as follows:

- 1 Infantry base: 300–500 men
- 1 Cavalry base: 125–200 mounts
- 1 Artillery base: 6–9 guns

In practice the number varies quite a lot and more detailed information can be found in the section *Using these rules for historical battles.*

BASING

Standard bases will be 60mm wide for 20-28mm figures, 40mm wide for 15mm figures and 30mm wide for 5 to 10 mm figures. Depth of base is recommended to be 45mm/30mm/20mm although this is less important and indeed is impossible for some Artillery models, depending on manufacturer and scale. Usually 'whatever fits' is the accepted norm.

Although the rules are designed to allow alternate base sizes to be used in the same battle, it is recommended that a standard base width should be used throughout a single army, as it will have benefits in being able to interchange attachments between units from game to game.

For example, using a standard base width for Artillery will enable the model to be used as either an attachment or as part of an Artillery unit. Using the same base width for Cavalry and Infantry will allow officer attachments to be used for both (although Cavalry officers often have quite different uniforms to Infantry officers).

INFANTRY

Within the troops termed as *Infantry* there were several types. Their tactical deployment and employment was similar at the demi-brigade and brigade level, even if their quality differed.

Line Infantry formed the majority infantry type in most armies. A line battalion often included a company of grenadiers, a company of *light infantry* (called voltigeurs by the French) and a variable number of line companies (often called musketeers). Individual companies are not modelled within the regimental or demi-brigade units used in the rules, but players are encouraged to use different bases or single ranks of figures within these larger formations to represent them.

Line Infantry are also further subdivided into 2 types of tactical formation which existed within the period. We refer to these as non-*reformed* and *reformed* based upon their nation's use of line (l'*ordre*

REFORMED AND UNREFORMED UNITS

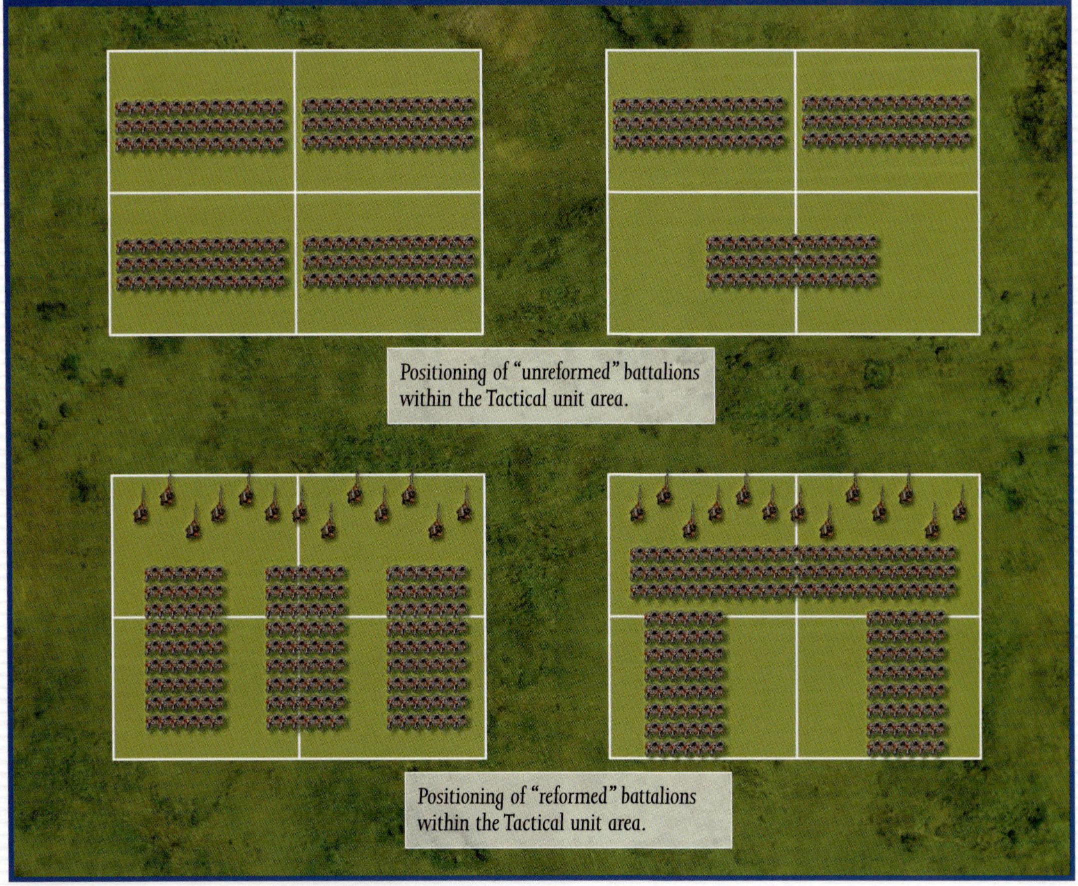

Positioning of "unreformed" battalions within the Tactical unit area.

Positioning of "reformed" battalions within the Tactical unit area.

mince) or *column (l'ordre profond)* for battlefield manoeuvre. The French adopted *l'ordre profound* at the start of the revolutionary wars and continued to use it throughout. The other main nations used *l'ordre mince* at the start of the period, only changing to *l'ordre profond* after their experiences against the French. Reformed troops typically introduced light infantry companies into their battalion formations.

Light Infantry were often trained to form up entirely in skirmish order. They should not be confused with skirmish companies, which could be deployed from almost any infantry unit. In the rules *light infantry* are represented by a mix of close and open order bases, with all bases being in open order if the entire unit is deployed into skirmish formation.

Riflemen were allocated to units in the Austrian Prussian and Russian armies as well as some of the German states. These were often known as 'schutzen' translated as 'shooters'. The Prussians had one 'schutzen' battalion, but it was more usual for riflemen to be allocated as companies. Usually only part of a unit had rifles. Even the British, who did give rifles to whole regiments, still deployed the men in individual companies attached to other battalions, regiments or brigades. Rifles had a longer range than smoothbore muskets, but a slower rate of fire.

Guard Infantry formations were used by most nations. The Austrians for example had none. The French and Russians in particular had whole corps of *Guards*, although most countries settled for a few battalions organised into divisions or sometimes just brigades. *Guards* were usually formed of the best troops in the army, but not all formations called *Guard* were of the same standard.

Conscripts were relied upon in some form by most armies for much of the period. The most notable exceptions were the British army and in the 1790s the 'ancien regimes'. But by the end of the period most armies had come to rely heavily on *Conscripts* to maintain the levels of their forces, again with the exception of the British. *Conscripts* would often receive training only after joining the army in the field. If they survived long enough they would, in time, receive enough training and experience to be considered *Drilled*, and eventually even *Veteran*.

Austrian Jæger

Russian Infantry

Standard sizes for all base types are:

- 20–28mm figures: 60mm wide x 45mm deep
- 12–18mm figures: 40mm wide x 30mm deep
- 5–10mm figures: 30mm wide by 20mm deep

Players using 10 or 12mm figures may use the either the 5–10mm or the 12–18mm bases as they prefer (see the section *'Optional Figure Basing'* for instructions on how to use different figure and base sizes for these rules)

INFANTRY UNIT ORGANISATION

Groups of single bases are placed together to form 'units'. The organisation of troops into larger formations differed during the course of the Napoleonic wars and from country to country. To use your bases of figures in these rules they must be combined to form units which will each represent several battalions, a single demi-brigade or regiment. Because unit strength varied greatly from nation to nation and even single nations at different times during the period, we have allowed the use of 2 different sizes of units: 'small' and 'large'. A small unit can be assumed to have a nominal strength of between 1,200 and 2,000 men, with a large unit being 2,000 to 3,000 men. In many cases this will be a full brigade of Infantry, but in others it will be less than a full brigade. For points based games you only 'buy' single units of either of the 2 sizes.

INFANTRY FORMATIONS

Until the late 18th century the **line** was the standard battlefield formation for Infantry but by the time of these wars the assault column came more into use and the hollow Square for defending against Cavalry.

However a column was not a deep formation with men shoulder to shoulder and many ranks deep like a pike phalanx. Individual platoons and companies would be organized in three ranks with intervals between them to their flank and rear. Intervals were necessary to enable changes of formation and the passage of officers. By the Napoleonic Wars even the fully deployed line was only 3 ranks deep – and sometimes only two.

A brigade was rarely deployed with all regiments in line abreast. The most common deployment was in line with multiple battalions behind each other, or in columns with battalions abreast. We refer to both of these formations as 'Tactical' formations and do not differentiate between them on the table top – assuming that the local officers in charge would use the most effective formation for the situation faced.

Units will most often be deployed in Tactical formation. This is shown by placing the unit bases 2 deep. Small units will be 2 bases wide and large units will be 3 bases wide.

Another type of Tactical formation is supported or self-supported. This is a deeper formation available only to large formations. It is shown by placing the bases 2 wide and 3 deep representing a large unit deployed on the same frontage as a small unit, but with much greater depth. The unit loses front rank firing capability in exchange for greater momentum in combat.

If a unit consists entirely of *light infantry* then half its bases (the front rank) should be shown as *Skirmisher* bases, with all other non-Skirmisher bases being also of *light infantry*. A unit of entirely *light infantry* may also be formed up entirely in *Skirmish* order, in which case all Infantry bases should be replaced by *Skirmisher* bases.

There will be times when a unit will need to move quickly around the battlefield. It will be able to do this much better if formed in 'March Column'. This formation is represented by placing a unit's bases 1 wide and 4 or 6 deep.

To maximise fire in a defensive position, an entire unit may choose to form up in 'Extended Line' formation, represented by placing the unit bases 4 or 6 wide and 1 deep.

Extended Lines can 'kink' at their centre point. If following a terrain feature this kink may be of any angle up to 90 degrees. Unless following a terrain feature the 2 halves of the unit may not 'bend' towards each other. After kinking both half-units must remain with their nearest corners touching.

The final formation that an Infantry unit may use is that of Square. Normally it is only used by Infantry if they are about to be attacked by Cavalry. This is shown by placing the unit in Tactical formation and turning the rear rank to face the rear.

A 2nd method of showing unit in Square formation is to turn the bases so that at least one is facing in each direction.

Spanish Guerrilla

CAVALRY

There are three basic types of Cavalry for use on a battlefield which are:

- **Battle or Heavy Cavalry:** Their main purpose was to engage enemy Cavalry, to assault Infantry en masse and to support their own Infantry either in attack or when defending. Heavy Cavalry included cavalry called dragoons in most nations, and cuirassiers in many. These were big men on big horses. They were equipped with long straight swords where the point and impetus was the key to the use of the weapon. They would usually canter into action, or might gallop only for a short distance as they closed on their enemy.
- **Light Cavalry:** Who can carry out the same functions, but, other than lancers, are less likely to assault Infantry. They were also used to guard the flanks of the army and to pursue a *Broken* enemy. They could turn a defeat into a massacre. Light Cavalry were smaller men on smaller horses and included hussars (perhaps the most flamboyant of the cavalry), chasseurs, chevaulegers and lancers. Confusingly, some nations had cavalry called dragoons who were really only light cavalry. By the end of the period most nations had introduced lancers (uhlans) whose principal target was enemy infantry.

NOTES ON TYPES OF CAVALRY

Irregular Cavalry are only found in some armies. These were mainly cossacks and uzbeks with the Russian army, Polish krakhaus and the Mameluks in Egypt. They were not usually present on battlefields and if present usually acted on the flanks as screens and scouts. The Ottoman army was an exception to this and used both heavy and light *irregular* cavalry in large numbers in most large battles.

Horse Guards could be heavy or light, lancers or cuirassiers. They functioned pretty much as all other cavalry but their light cavalry would usually be used in the same way and often at the same time as the heavy cavalry.

Shock Cavalry were the heaviest cavalry of the period. These were usually comprised of the biggest men on the biggest horses. Most cuirassiers fall into this category, but there are others: Carabiniers and mounted grenadiers being typical examples. The definition of which Cavalry can be 'shock' is specified in our companion army lists.

FIREARMS AND CAVALRY

Firearms were seldom used on horseback on the battlefield in an organised manner. Cavalry would occasionally skirmish with each other using their carbines and pistols and might also use them in melee, but there would be no chance to reload and there was no drill for using them en masse. Cavalry did not routinely dismount to fight in a battle and where there is historical justification for dismounted cavalry in battle, they are given a suitable infantry classification.

CAVALRY UNIT ORGANISATION

In these rules a small unit has an assumed strength of between 500 and 800 men, with a large unit being 800 to 1200 men. Often this will be a full brigade, but could also be a regiment or a group of squadrons perhaps from more than one regiment.

Units will most often be deployed in Tactical formation. This is shown by placing the unit bases 2 deep. Small units will be 2 bases wide and large units will be 3 bases wide.

Large units may also be deployed in a deeper self-supported Tactical formation, by placing the bases 3 deep and 2 wide.

Another formation used by cavalry is that of Extended Line. This is most often used by skirmishing light or *irregular* light cavalry:

Cavalry can also form March Column. This is represented by placing the bases in a column 1 base wide. March Column is mainly used to quickly redeploy Cavalry to another part of the battlefield.

CAVALRY FORMATIONS

For cavalry the line was the preferred formation for a charge. References to cavalry columns misunderstand their formation which was essentially a column of lines one behind the other again with intervals, usually each line being one regiment 2-3 ranks deep. This is the standard tactical formation for cavalry.

Austrian Artilleryman

ARTILLERY

In this period artillery came into its own on the battlefield, and the ratio of guns to men rose markedly and they came to cause more casualties than small arms by a factor of about 4:3. There were two basic types of field piece.

The first type was the long barrelled smooth bore muzzle-loading **cannon,** measured by the weight of shot – 3, 4, 6, 8, 9 and 12 pounders were all used. Cannon had a low elevation and generally fired on a flat trajectory and could not be depressed much with ease.

The second type was the **howitzer,** also smooth bore but short and stubby with a wide bore and a higher angle of elevation. Most nations' batteries had a mix of cannon and howitzers 1:2 or 1:3. Howitzers could be fired from just behind a crest or in a slight depression, but purely indirect fire was not used.

There were two types of artillery unit. Most were termed **Field Artillery.** In essence the gunners walked or marched alongside the guns and their limbers, ammunition caissons, etc. The second was **Horse Artillery** where the gunners rode either on horses or on the limbers themselves. Usually *horse artillery* had the lighter weights of guns: typically 6pdrs. They too could have howitzers.

Artillery models are often difficult to place on a 'standard' depth base. We therefore allow the bases to be 60mm/40mm/30mm deep – or more – to accommodate the models. However, heavy artillery will always be on a base at least 60mm/40mm/30mm deep to represent the space taken up by the additional caissons required to support them.

When limbered, Artillery units can be replaced by a single Limber model. This should be on a base 40mm wide and up to 90mm deep (120mm for a large unit). In practice, it may be expedient to use the artillery models themselves 'in column' to show that they are limbered.

TACTICAL USE OF ARTILLERY

The type of pieces used and ordnance fired did not, as such, determine how Artillery was used on the field of battle.

Position Artillery was deliberately placed in a position where it could bring sustained fire at longer ranges onto massed or large enemy targets. Field and horse artillery could both be used as position artillery but horse less commonly. All Artillery in separate units are position artillery.

Support Artillery was common and was essentially Artillery assigned to individual infantry or cavalry formations. Typically they would deployed in the line with the infantry in defensive positions or move forward with the infantry or cavalry and deployed in positions of tactical advantage close to enemy – in grape range if possible. All artillery attachments are support artillery.

Fire by Prolong was a method of manhandling artillery forward by the use of 'prolongs' or 'scheiplel' – long thick ropes with hooks and eyelets – or by the use of handspikes. It was not always necessary or even practical to limber and unlimber guns and even quite heavy field artillery could be advanced in this way.

Regimental and Battalion Guns were used by some armies at times during period. They were generally ineffective in larger scale actions and often as not were lost on campaign as the logistical challenges to sustain them grew too great.

Horse Artillery, when used other than as support artillery for cavalry or infantry, was a highly mobile reserve to convert success to victory or recover from a setback. Horse artillery could not fire any better or faster than their field counterparts gun for gun but they could rapidly move around the battle field to take up key positions. **Grand or massed Batteries** became much more common as the period went on and grew to be up to 200 pieces strong. They would be less likely to be used in an action at Corps level which is the 'standard' for these rules. Players will be allowed to use larger batteries in larger multi-corps battles.

French Artillery officer

ARTILLERY UNIT ORGANISATION

In these rules an artillery unit is used to represent a number of guns of greater than single battery size and are usually used to provide long range support for the Infantry and Cavalry units (i.e. position artillery.) A small unit represents 12 and 19 guns while a large unit represents 20 to 30 guns. There are 2 modes of deployment: limbered and unlimbered.

LIMBERED ARTILLERY

When moving around the battlefield artillery units should be shown in their limbered formation. To do this remove the unlimbered artillery pieces and replace them with a single base containing an artillery limber. For small units this will be of 4 draught horses. For large batteries it should either have 6 draught horses or should have 4 horses, but carry an artillery piece behind it.

ATTACHMENTS

In order to bring out further differences in capabilities and strengths of units, we use 'attachments'. An attached base is a base that replaces one of the standard bases in the unit and has figures and models on it representing some added capability.

There are 4 different attachments that may be use:

SKIRMISHERS

Most reformed infantry units have integral light companies to provide a nominal Skirmish capability. This is reflected in a unit's ability to fire at the 6MU Skirmish range. Some units do not have this capability.

Some regiment sized units have a large number of light infantry within their formation, over and above the normal light companies with individual battalions. This may be either entire battalions of light troops, or additional companies of light troops attached for the duration of the battle. In this case the unit will be allowed to take a *Skirmisher* attachment.

The *Skirmisher* base should be placed at the front of the unit in the left most position. Where the attachment is justified because the unit is of mixed line and *light infantry*, the base immediately behind the *Skirmisher* base should be of *light infantry* if the unit is in Tactical formation, as shown below.

For those players who prefer to see their Skirmish line out in front of the main battle line we have an alternate method of representing them, although all measurement distances for movement firing, etc. are made from the main unit. The Skirmish bases are ignored for all game purposes, other than as an indication that the parent body contains *light infantry* and should be repositioned as necessary if they obstruct the movement of any other unit or base.

ARTILLERY

As we have already described, some infantry units were allocated a small number of regimental or battalion light artillery guns for support purposes and these are already factored into the unit. However, sometimes formations were allocated additional guns from divisional or corps reserve and we build this into the rules by allowing units to add Artillery attachments. Models used to represent these may be either foot or horse Artillery, although for accuracy attachments to Cavalry units should always be depicted as *horse artillery*. Note that attached Artillery in an Infantry unit cannot fire independently unless their parent unit is unreformed and the target is at medium range.

Note that Artillery units can have Artillery attachments. In this case however a base is not replaced; the attachment is simply added alongside the existing bases. This will increase the frontage of the unit. These attachments may be of additional medium artillery, heavy artillery, howitzers or rockets.

When using artillery on bases that are deeper than the standard, they should be placed with either the front edge or the rear edge of the unit aligned. The choice makes no difference in game turns, since all measurements are made as if they were aligned with front edge of the Infantry.

British Commander

OFFICERS

Some units may be led by additional officers or by an officer who is of outstanding ability. To represent this we use optional *Brigade Commander* attachments. He behaves in every way like a *Division Commander* except that he has no *Command Points* and only affects, and may not leave, the unit he has been attached to. He also has an increased chance of becoming a casualty. His base is normally placed in the centre of the front rank if possible.

CAVALRY

Occasionally an infantry unit had a small number (usually a company) of cavalry attached to the brigade. We therefore allow some units to have Cavalry attachments. Their main value was in driving off enemy skirmishers.

It always replaces the base that is most to the rear and most to the right of a unit.

RESTRICTIONS

The maximum number of attachments a unit can have is restricted by the size, the basing and the type of unit. These restrictions are described as follows:

- An Artillery unit may only have an attachment of artillery.
- A Cavalry unit may only have artillery and officer attachments.
- An Infantry unit (whether large or small) may have a maximum of 2 attachments. It is possible that a small *light infantry* unit has all of its front rank bases replaced with attachments. If this occurs the opposing player must be informed when the unit is first placed on the table.

COMMANDERS

To control your forces on the battlefield you will need to use your Commanders.

Commanders are the only bases in your army that are independent bases and hence are allowed to move on their own. *Corps Commanders* and *Division Commanders* are based as follows:

- 20–28mm: 60mm x 60mm
- 12–18mm: 40mm x 40mm
- 5–10mm: 30mm x 30mm

Both *Divisional* and *Corps Commanders* may optionally be on 60mm/40mm/30mm diameter circular bases, or by choice may be on the same base depth as an attached *Commander* base.

POINTS SYSTEM

Players who wish to design their own armies should use the points values given in the *Points Cost* table. Totals points used for a battle lasting from 3 to 4 hours should be around 800 per player, although up to 1200 points per player can easily be handled with experience. This should normally be enough to field a corps of 2 to 4 divisions. Points are charged for each base of a unit, with units consisting of 2 or 3 bases for Artillery and 4 or 6 bases for Infantry and Cavalry units. Attachments are paid for separately and will replace an already paid for base of an existing Infantry or Cavalry unit, or be added to the 2 or 3 bases of an Artillery unit. Field fortifications, if used, cost a fixed number of points for depending on their size. A small fortification can only be defended by a small unit, while a large one can be defended by both small and large units.

Points Cost (per base)	**Training**				**Élan Bonus**	
Troop Type	**Veteran**	**Drilled**	**Conscript**	Irregular	Superior	Poor
Infantry						
Line Infantry (non-reformed)	10	8	6	7	3	-2
Line Infantry (reformed)	13	10	7	-	4	-2
Light Infantry	16	12	9	8	5	-3
Cavalry						
Light Cavalry	10	8	6	7	3	-1
Heavy cavalry	13	10	8	9	4	-2
Artillery						
Medium Foot	28	20	-	-	4	-4
Heavy Foot and Howitzers	32	24	-	-	7	-5
Horse Artillery	32	24	-	-	6	-5

Attachments		**Special Capabilities**		**Commanders**	
Skirmishers with muskets	8	Rifles	1	Exceptional commander	80
Skirmishers with rifles	10	Guards	4	Skilled commander	50
Medium Artillery, Rockets	10	Lancers	2	Competent commander	30
Heavy Artillery, Howitzers	12	Shock	3	Charismatic commander	+10
Officer attachment	12	Impetuous	-1	Allied commander	-10
Cavalry attachment	6	Immobile Artillery	-5	Fieldworks Small/Large	20/30

SETTING UP A POINTS BASED GAME

PRE-BATTLE INITIATIVE

The *most successful generals* in history endeavoured to bring the enemy to battle in a place of their choosing, whether they were the invader, or were in defence of their own territory. Often they achieved this through better battlefield intelligence, which often gave them the initiative in the forthcoming battle. In *Field of Glory Napoleonic* we reflect this by allowing the general who has gained this initiative to select the overall terrain region, reflecting the likelihood that he will have a greater influence on choosing the battlefield. His opponent also starts deploying first, revealing his initial dispositions while the player with the initative is also allowed to make the first move. However, just as in reality, a good opponent will devise his own tactics to counter these advantages.

Before set up each player rolls a D6 and adds his total initiative modifier. If the total scores are equal, roll again. The high scorer has pre-battle initiative.

Initiative rating is a combination of 3 factors: The skill level of the *Corps Commander* of the army. A value assigned to the army in the list for that army. A dice roll modifier.

CALCULATING YOUR INITIATIVE VALUE

- Start with the skill level of the *Corps Commander* of your army.
- Add to this the initiative value of your army for that year.
- Add to this the score of a single dice roll.

The player with the higher score is the attacker and the other player is the defender. If the scores are level then both players must roll the dice again and recalculate.

If the attacker has an initiative score of at least 3 higher than his opponent, he gains an additional 1 or 2 units of either Infantry or Cavalry. The extra unit(s) can be of any type or size, but must not exceed 40pts in value. These extra troops must be added to an existing command, (which must also be deployed on-table) and the choice of Infantry or Cavalry (or both) must be made immediately after dicing for initiative. The unit(s) may not create a 'mixed' division from an otherwise non-mixed one. The choice of unit(s) must be announced to the defender. The attacker's Army Combat Value (ACV) does not change for adjudicating victory, but the defender has an extra 2 points added to his. This means that the attacker must cause an additional point of damage to defeat the defender. It should also be noted that each player must provide for the bonus unit(s) in addition to those units forming his predesigned army. If an army list does not contain any bases costing 10 points or less, the 40pts may be spend on an additional 2 bases, converting an existing small unit into a large unit.

The attacker will deploy 2nd and will make the first move in the game. During the first 2 moves of the game there are restrictions on movement as follows:

- The attacker may not make a 'move to the rear' with any of his units other than those in Skirmish order, or as a result of on outcome move.
- The defender may not move any of his units other than *Skirmishers* to a position outside his deployment area except as follows:
  - To counter-charge with Cavalry.
  - As a result of an outcome move.
  - To advance no more than one normal move distance to enter or move into contact with buildings.

TERRAIN

Players sit opposite each other, with each taking the nearest edge of the table as his base edge. For standard games this will be one of the longer edges of the table.

All references to 'own' edge or half of the table refer to the side of the table nearest to the player concerned.

Each army list in our companion army list books specifies a set of territory types characteristic of those typically found in the army's region of activity. The player gaining the initiative MUST choose a region available to both armies. If no region is common to both armies he chooses a region from his opponent's available options. Terrain is then chosen and placed according to this territory type.

The table below shows the terrain pieces available in each territory type. The maximum number of allowed pieces of each type is shown, followed by the compulsory minimum in brackets. Both players make their terrain selections from the row relating to the territory type chosen by the player with pre-battle initiative.

ALLOWED TERRAIN TYPES PER REGION

Region	Open	Steep Hill	Gentle hill	River or Stream	Road	Impassable	Difficult	Buildings	Rough/ Cover
France & Central Europe	1	2	4(1)	1	3(1)	0	2	4(1)	3(1)
Southern Europe	0	3(1)	3	1	3(1)	1	3(1)	3	3(1)
Spain & Portugal	1	4(2)	4(1)	1	2	1	3(1)	2	2
Eastern Europe	2(1)	2	4(1)	1	2	1	3(1)	2	4(1)
Egypt & Middle East	4(1)	1	3(1)	1	2(1)	0	4	2	3(1)

TERRAIN DESCRIPTION, VISIBILITY AND COMBAT EFFECTS

Open

An open area of ground offering no impediment to movement. All areas of the table not covered by other terrain is considered to be open. It has no effect on visibility

River or stream

A river must be 2 to 4MU wide and a stream must be more than 1/2MU and less than 2MU wide. A river's length is determined by the placement rules. In Egypt and the Middle East a river may have dried up in which case it is classified as a gulley for its entire length. A river can only have 1 bend of up to 90deg. It has no effect on visibility. The strength of flow is diced for at placement.

Road

A road should be of a width to accommodate your figures when moving in 'March Column'. This will normally be 40mm. It may include 1 bend and may not be longer than the table's longest edge.

- A road cannot touch the edge of the table within 12MU of another road.
- If there is at least one building that does not have a road passing through or touching it, then any road placed must pass through or touch at least one of these buildings.
- If all buildings have at least one road passing through or touching them, then a road must pass through or touch a building or another road if there is one.
- A road crossing a river must have a bridge or a ford at the crossing point.

Area Features

An area feature may be one of 2 sizes:

- Normal piece: A 4" x 6" (10cm x 15cm) rectangle can be fitted entirely within its footprint. Its entire footprint can be fitted within a 12" (300mm) diameter circle.
- Large piece: A 4" x 6" rectangle can be fitted entirely within its footprint. Its footprint cannot be entirely fitted within a 12" diameter circle. Its entire footprint can be fitted within a 16" (40cm) diameter circle. A large piece counts as 2 selections and as 2 towards the maximum of that type, except that a compulsory item only counts as 1 selection regardless of size.

Steep Hills

These can be steep, or partially steep. A steep hill can also have the following superimposed: A wood or plantation, a building, rough ground.

The steep section of a partially steep hill must be clearly identifiable and must be a single section that cannot extend around nor cover more than half of the hill. A partially steep hill is counted a steep hill selection if small and both a gentle hill and a steep hill selection if large. A hill with another superimposed area feature counts as the terrain equivalent of both. For example, a large hill with a small plantation on it would count as 3 terrain selections. A large steep hill can only have a large superimposed area feature if one them is compulsory, it then counts as 3 selections. The steep section of a hill is always difficult going and the non-steep section is 'open'. Note that any other superimposed terrain may override this.

A hill blocks line of sight. Troops on the near side of an otherwise 'open' hill can be seen from any distance. Visibility of troops on a 'covered' hill is the same as the rules for the type of cover. Troops within 2MU of the crest of an 'open' hill can see other troops over the crest at any distance, but can only be seen in return if the enemy are within 6MU of the crest. Infantry may fire over the crest of a hill at medium range. Both Artillery and Infantry may fire over the crest of a hill at close range.

Gentle Hill

A gentle hill is treated exactly the same as a steep hill, except that it is counted as open over its entire area. Note that any other superimposed terrain may override this.

Rough Ground

This terrain type covers any terrain that inhibits movement in formation, but does not provide cover from firing, except if the unit is behind, and in contact, with walls or hedges surrounding an enclosed field. This terrain type would include open or

TERRAIN SIZES

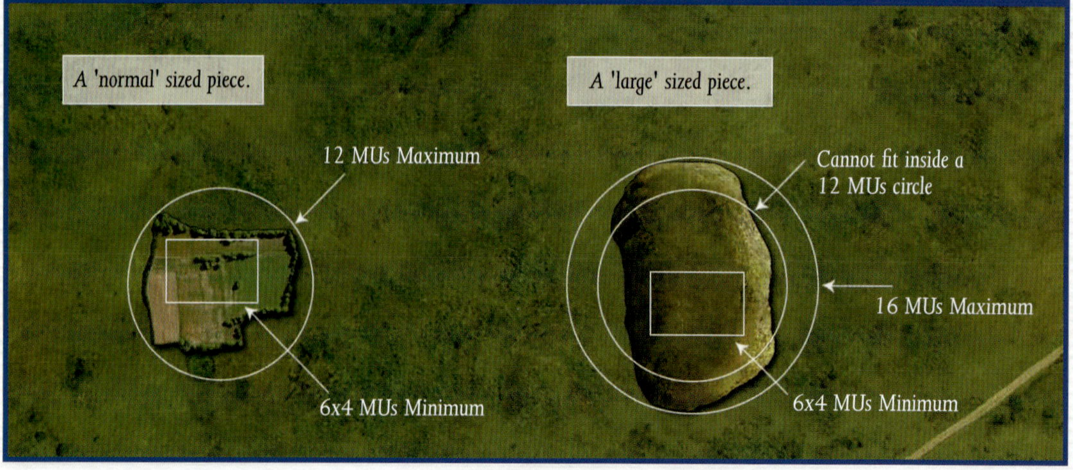

enclosed fields, rocky ground or an area of brush. It could also include areas of soft sand. It has no effect on visibility.

Gulley

This terrain type is also 'Rough ground' and is an area of ground that is lower than that of the surrounding area. The whole area is treated as rough, but has special effects with regard to shooting and visibility.

Artillery wholly inside a gulley may not fire out. Infantry wholly inside a gulley may not fire out at close range, but may fire at medium range as normal. Both Infantry and Artillery may fire at any range at enemy units partially in the same gulley, or in contact with the gulley edge.

Troops partially inside a gulley fire in or out as if entirely in rough ground. Infantry outside the gulley can fire at troops inside at medium range as normal, but can only fire at close range if they are touching the edge. Artillery outside a gulley cannot fire at units entirely in the gulley unless they are touching the edge. Troops outside a gulley can see troops inside when within 6MU of the edge of it. Units entirely inside a gulley count as being in cover, units partially in a gulley count as being in the open. A gulley is considered to be cover and may be chosen as part of the rough/cover selections.

Cover

This terrain type could be, rough or difficult ground but always provides cover for troops in it. It may also block line of sight. Examples would be open woods, plantations and vineyards. Troops wholly inside can only be seen at 6MU range, unless they are firing out. Troops inside fire as if in difficult, but fight as if in rough. Troops beyond cover cannot be seen through or over it, even from a hill.

Difficult

Terrain of this type makes movement in formation very difficult, if not impossible. It may also give cover and block line of sight. Examples would be marsh, dense woods and steep slopes.

A marsh has no effect on visibility. Troops in a dense wood can only be seen from 2MU unless firing, and also count as in cover. Troops beyond woods cannot be seen through or over it, even from a hill.

Impassable

This would block movement of troops entirely and may also block line of sight. The 2 most common types would be a lake or a rocky outcrop. Their placement is heavily restricted. Troops cannot enter and are destroyed if forced into it. A lake does not block visibility, but troops beyond other types of impassable cannot be seen through or over it, even from a hill.

Buildings

These are a special terrain feature and give special privileges to troops entering them. A building may only a small sized terrain feature, but it is possible that 2 or more buildings could be placed adjacent to each other, to create a larger village or collection of buildings. A building area can contain a single infantry unit.

There are special rules for firing and fighting troops in buildings (see '*special features*') When a building is occupied by a unit it will have bases either in, or around the outside of the feature. Buildings block line of sight, although they can be seen to be occupied or defended from any distance.

TERRAIN SELECTION

- The player who is the defender selects a **small** hill of one of the selected region's compulsory type(s) and places this on the table in any location entirely in his own centre section. If his opponent has received 1 or 2 additional units because of pre-battle initiative the defender may increase the size of this **small** hill to a **large** one. He next places a straight road running from any point of the edge of his own centre sector directly to any point of his opponent's rear edge and centre sector. These are in addition to any terrain selected during the rest of the placement sequence. No dice rolls are required and they may not be moved by the attacker.

- The attacker then selects 2 of the 4 compulsory pieces and must choose a **village** if the territory region is France or Central Europe.
- The defender must select the other 2 compulsory pieces.
- The attacker then takes between 2 to 4 other optional selections from the list of available terrain. The total pieces of any type, together with any compulsory features of that type, cannot exceed the maximum of that type.
- The defender then makes his 2 to 4 other optional selections from the list of available terrain. He cannot select any pieces that, together with those already chosen by both players, would exceed the maximum of that type.
- Note that a compulsory hill with another compulsory terrain selection superimposed will use up 2 of the player's compulsory terrain selections.

All terrain selections are made before **any** are placed on the table.

TERRAIN PLACEMENT SEQUENCE

The order in which terrain is placed is as follows:

1. If any player chooses a ***river*** or ***stream*** this is deployed first.
2. Players now place their selected terrain pieces (other than roads) alternately until all pieces have been placed (or discarded) starting with the defender. ***Compulsory items*** (other than roads) must be placed before any non-compulsory items.
3. Both players place any remaining roads – defender first.
4. The defender places any field fortifications anywhere in the centre sector of his own deployment area. No dice roll is made for placement and his opponent may not roll to move it. The attacker may not place any field fortifications.

A river (or stream) is placed as follows:
The player placing the river rolls a dice:

- 1–3 The river enters on a flank sector of his opponent's long edge at least 8MU from the side edge.
- 4–5 The river enters on a flank sector of his own long edge at least 8MU from the side edge.
- 6 The river is discarded.

The same player then rolls a 2nd dice

- 1–3 The river leaves the table on a side edge of the same flank in his opponent's half of the table at least 8MU from the long edge.
- 4–6 The river leaves the table on a side edge of the same flank in the player's own half of the table at least 8MU from the long edge.

The strength of the river is checked as follows:

After placement his opponent rolls a d6, subtracting 2 for a stream (less than 1MU wide) and subtracting 1 if the region is Egypt/Middle East. Subtract 3 for a stream in Egypt/Middle East.

- 1 or less Water is ankle deep – No effect on movement. If the region is Egypt & Middle East, a selected river or stream has dried up.
- 2–3 Water is waist high – units may cross if passing a CMT
- 4–5 Water is shoulder high – May only cross with a commander and must still pass a CMT.
- 6 Surging torrent – cannot be crossed except at bridge or ford.

TERRAIN PLACEMENT DICE ROLLS

No piece can be placed (prior to adjustment) within 4MU of any other piece except:

- Any piece can be placed closer than 4MU to a river a stream or a road.
- A road can be placed closer than 4MU to any piece and can pass through a building, or over a hill, stream or river but not through other terrain pieces.
- A building may be placed adjacent to another building to represent a larger village or collection of buildings. It may also be placed entirely on a gentle hill. It may be moved as normal by the opposing player.

The placing player rolls to determine where on the table a piece is to be placed. The other player then makes an adjustment roll, which may allow the placement to be amended or negated. During initial placement the entire piece must be within the designated sector(s).

The placement roll:

- 1 Touching opponent's long edge.
- 2 Touching his own long edge.
- 3 Touching any side edge – Entire terrain piece must be over 8MU from any long edge.
- 4 Anywhere over 8MU from edges – entirely in opponent's half.
- 5 Anywhere over 8MU from edges – entirely in player's own half.
- 6 Anywhere straddling the centre line with at least 2MU in both players' halves.

The initial placement roll is not required for rivers, streams or roads.

The placement roll is halved for impassable terrain (rounding up – i.e. 1–2 becomes a 1, a 3– 4 becomes a 2, a 5–6 becomes a 3).

The adjustment roll is made after each terrain feature is placed:

TERRAIN PLACEMENT

- 0–2 No change permitted.
- 3–4 Can slide the piece up to 6MU in any direction.
- 5 Can either slide the piece up to 12MU in any direction or pivot the piece on one point through any angle.
- 6+ Can remove the piece entirely.

Modify the die roll by:

- -1 if the piece is a compulsory terrain item.
- +1 if it is impassable.

When a piece 'slides' it must maintain its angle of placement relative to the table edges. To pivot, fix any point on the edge of the terrain piece and rotate the piece around this point. A piece cannot be slid or pivoted off table, nor to overlap another terrain piece, but may end within 4MU of any other piece and can ignore sector boundaries. A piece cannot be slid to with 4MU of a table edge if it was not permitted to be placed within 4MU to begin with.

DEPLOYMENT

Note that where an army list indicates that attachments must be allocated after terrain placement and before deployment – this is the time to allocate those attachments.

Deployment zones are as follows:

- Defender: anywhere up to 6MU from the centreline.
- Attacker: anywhere up to 10MU from the centreline.

After terrain has been placed the players now deploy as follows:

1. The attacker may choose to flank-march with one of his Divisions. He must make a note of the division, the flank, and the sector that it will appear from.
2. Defender places his LOC.
3. Attacker places his LOC.
4. Players deploy their commands alternately, 3 units at a time, starting with the defender. The units must be placed in command order. That is, once a unit is placed, all other units in its command must therefore be placed before a unit from a different command can be deployed.
5. *Commanders* are placed as soon as all units in their command have been placed. They do not count towards the '3 units at a time'.
6. As units are placed on the table, the owner must fully define their troop type, training, élan, and weapons.
7. Either player may choose not to place the whole of his last deployed Division on the table, and instead bring it on during the game as a 'Reserve'. He must make a note of the sector that it will appear from.
8. Once a player has placed all the units of his on-table divisions, if he has any commands off-table, he should place a single commander base adjacent to, or as close as possible to his LOC. He should place any notes defining his flank-march and/or reserve under this base.

Note that where an army list indicates that attachments must be allocated after deployment - this is the time to allocate those attachments.

PLACING FIELD FORTIFICATIONS

These may only be used in a points based game by prior agreement or if permitted by the army list if choosing an army from one of our accompanying army list books. They can only be placed by the defender, immediately after terrain has been placed and before any units are placed. They may be placed anywhere in the defender's deployment area, at least 8MU from a table edge. See *Special features/field fortifications*.

ATTACHMENTS

Some armies are more flexible with the allocation of attachments than others.

If using our accompanying army list books, there will be restrictions on how and when attachments can be allocated. Most attachments will be allocated to their units when the army is created. Some attachments will be allocated to divisions, but not to units. In this case the attachments should be allocated to units by the player as his units are placed on the table. In the most flexible armies, the British being a typical example, attachments may be placed after deployment. In this case the player should deploy his units without attachments, and only replace his *normal* bases with attachments after both armies have been deployed.

FLANK MARCHES AND RESERVES

The player with the initiative may send one of his divisions on a *flank march*. The decision of whether or not to make a *flank march* is made after all terrain has been placed, but before the first unit is placed on the table. The player should make a note of the flank and sector from which it will arrive (Right or Left & Front or Rear – rear being his own half of the table).

Either player may choose to deploy a whole division in reserve off-table. This decision may be made at any time during deployment, as long as no unit of the reserve division has been placed. He should make a note of the sector from which it will arrive (Right, Left or Centre).

After all other troops have been deployed, each player with a command off-table places the note(s) made under his LOC.

Instructions for bringing reserves and flank marches onto the table are explained under *Moving reserves and flank marches onto the table.*

GLOSSARY OF TERMS

GLOSSARY OF TERMS

<: Less than.

<=: Less than or equal to.

>: Greater than.

>=: Greater than or equal to.

Active Player: The player whose turn it currently is.

Advance: Any move which results in at least part of the unit ending further forwards than the original front edge and facing.

Artillery: Any unit or attachment that has a gun model on it. Units may be: *heavy, medium* or *mortar*. An Artillery attachment may also be *howitzer* or *rocket*. Artillery units are also classified as either *foot artillery* or *horse artillery*.

Assault Range: A unit of Infantry or Cavalry is in assault range if any part of a front edge or front corner can contact enemy within its normal move distance.

Attachment: An attachment is used to indicate that a unit has an additional level of combat or firing ability. 1 or 2 bases of a unit may be replaced with one of the following 4 attachment types: Skirmishers, Artillery, Cavalry or Officer (Brigade Commander). Artillery attachments for Infantry and Cavalry may only be medium. Artillery units may have attachments of other types of artillery or officers, but only as specified in their army list

Attacker: The player who wins the initiative at the start of the game. He deploys second and moves first. He may also gain additional troops.

Attrition Points: Attrition points are received for various adverse events, such as *Broken* or *Spent* units and Abandoned Guns and losing your LOC. If sufficient attrition points are accumulated, the army is Defeated. See the *Victory and Defeat* section.

Base Width: The width of a 'standard' base as used in these rules. This base width is the same even if using figure based for other rules; see the section *Using Figures Based for Other Rule Sets.*

The base width for different figure scales is:

- 20–28mm: 60mm
- 12–18mm: 40mm
- 5–10mm: 30mm

Brigade Group: A group of 2 or more units

French Hussars

moving together under the command and joined by their *Division Commander*. The number of units able to do so is equal to the commander's skill level +1.

Cavalry: Covers all types of mounted troops including Dragoons, Hussars, and Cuirassier etc. An attachment of Artillery does not affect the unit type. There are 2 basic types of Cavalry - Heavy and Light. All other types, such as Lancers will fall into 1 of these 2 basic types. Some of the heavy Cavalry may also be *Shock*.

Close Range: The range at which Infantry musketry fire by formed units is assumed to occur. For all firing this is <= 2MU.

Combat: A general term for fighting between units in contact with each other, at least one of which must be in contact with its front edge or front corner. Once such a combat has been joined, units are deemed to be in close combat until one side breaks off or is destroyed.

Cohesion Test (CT): A test taken to see if adverse events cause a unit to lose it's cohesion. Possible cohesion states are: Steady, Disordered, Wavering and *Broken*. See the *Morale and Recovery Mechanism* section.

Column: See 'March Column'.

Command range: The distance at which commanders can influence troops. It is the range at which he can control *Brigade Groups*, permit units under his command to perform complex moves and affect *Cohesion Tests*. *Corps Commanders* and *Division Commanders* have different ranges as follows:

	Corps Commander	Division Commander
Normal	20MU	8MU
Leading a unit	10MU	4MU
Leading a unit in combat	0MU	0MU

A *Brigade Commander* can only control his own unit. He therefore has an effective Command Range of 0MU

Command point: One *Command Point* is expended by a *Division Commander* for every *Complex Move Test* taken by a unit under his command. Both *Brigade* and *Division Commanders* each have a 'free' *Command Point* to be used only for a test taken by the unit or *Brigade Group* he is leading.

Complex Move Test (CMT): A test taken to see if a unit or *Brigade Group* can make a complex move as defined in the Complex Moves Table. See the *Complex Move Test* section of the General Rules.

Cover: The following terrain is considered to provide cover to bases entirely within them: Plantation, Woods, Vineyards, the edges of Enclosed Fields, and Buildings. Special rules for Historical games and Scenarios may allow other terrain types to be used which could provide cover.

1 Dice per x: 'Lose 1 dice per x' = Lose 1 dice per full x dice. That is, round dice up.

Deep Formation: A large unit of either Infantry or Cavalry placed 2 bases wide and 3 bases deep. It fires and fights as a small unit, but will still count as a large unit for reducing the number of hits on it by 1. A large unit in deep formation also provides rear support for itself.

Defended Obstacle: A piece of terrain defined as an obstacle (see *Special Features)* which has a non-*Broken* Infantry or Artillery unit either in it or with its front edge in contact with it. It does not count as 'defended' if there is an enemy unit capable of assaulting the defenders in the flank or rear during the next enemy Assault Phase.

Defended Building: Can only be defended by Infantry units. These must be placed facing outwards around the edge of the terrain piece (see *Special Features / Buildings*).

Defensive Position: Behind or in a *Buildings* or a *Defended Obstacle*, or if uphill of all enemy units a charge from any enemy would be at a disadvantage in combat for being 'enemy downhill'.

Élan: A measure of the quality of units. These are: *Superior*, *Average* and *Poor*. For combat and *Cohesion Tests* some of the dice may be re-rolled for *Superior* and *Poor* troops.

Élan Re-rolls: The mechanism by which the effect of troop quality is represented. Re-rolls in combat and for *Cohesion Tests* are as follows:

- Superior Guard: may re-roll 1s & 2s
- Superior units: may re-roll 1s
- Guard: may re-roll 1s
- Poor troops: MUST re-roll 6s

Extended line: See *Single Rank.*

Evade: A retire move used by Skirmishers to avoid being assaulted by the enemy. See the *General Movement Rules* section.

Field Fortifications: Earthworks, small redoubts or other obstacles used to improve a defensive position. See the *Special Features* section.

File: A single front rank base and all the bases of the same unit lined up behind it.

Flank March: A flank march may be attempted by a division in an attempt to catch the enemy off-balance by entering from a side edge and sector. It can only be used by a single division of the player who gains the initiative (see the *Pre-Battle Initiative* section).

Fresh Cavalry: Any Cavalry unit that is *unSpent* and not currently in combat.

Infantry: Covers all types of foot troops including line, light, guard, marines, dismounted dragoons, etc. There are 2 basic types of Infantry – Line and Light. All other types will fall into 1 of these 2 basic types. Depending on the nationality and date, they will also be either 'reformed' or 'unreformed'.

Interception Range: The distance at which Infantry and Cavalry can intercept an enemy assault. Infantry can only intercept Infantry, Cavalry can intercept any unit. The intercept distance is 2MU for Infantry and 4MU for Cavalry.

Irregular: Any unit of Infantry or Cavalry that is considered to have had no formal training in battlefield formations and tactics. It takes CMTs with only 1 dice, and re-roll 6s when firing. *Irregular* light Cavalry are always treated as *Skirmishers.*

Howitzers: A relatively short cannon that delivers shells at a medium muzzle velocity, usually by a high trajectory. They can only be used as attachments to other Artillery units.

Leading: A commander leading a unit improves the unit's re-roll by one when the unit is in combat. He also provides a 'free' CP when the unit takes a CMT. A Commander is always considered to be leading the unit he is in contact with.

Line of Command: All troops in a single division have as their line of command their own *Division Commander* and their *Corps Commander.* For larger battles there may also be an *Army Commander* in their line of command.

Line of Communications (LOC): A base placed on the table that represents the point on the table where an army receives its supply. If an army's LOC is occupied by the enemy, all the units in that army will add 1 to the dice rolled for *Cohesion Tests.*

Long Range: The range at which Artillery is assumed to be firing round shot, shell, etc. For all firing this is >6MU and <=16MU.

March Column: A unit of Infantry or Cavalry in a formation that is entirely 1 base wide.

Medium Range: The range at which Artillery fire canister and also the range at which *Skirmishers* are assumed to operate. For all firing the distance is > 2MU and <= 6MU.

Mortars: These will normally only be used in special scenarios and sieges, although sometimes used by Ottoman armies and others in the field. They would most often be deployed in or behind fieldworks.

Movement Units (MU): All distances are specified in *Movement Units* (MU). An MU varies depending on the scale of figures used in the game and may be metric or imperial as agreed by the players or decided by umpires or tournament organisers. See *Measurements.*

Non-reformed Infantry: See *Unreformed Infantry.*

Obstacle: Any piece of terrain that gives the unit a bonus in combat when placed in or behind it (see *Special Features*). These would include:

- Buildings
- Walls
- Thick hedges
- River banks
- Field fortifications
- Any other piece of terrain as defined by the umpire/game organiser, or if agreed by both players before the game starts.

Occupied: Applies to buildings and to LOCs. See *Line of Communications* for detailed rules for when this is occupied.

See *Special Features/Buildings* for rules on when these are considered occupied.

Open Terrain: The whole battlefield which is not covered by terrain is considered to be 'open'. A gentle hill is also considered to be 'open' if there is no other terrain superimposed on it.

Points of Advantage (POA): POA are combat advantages arising from troop type, combat capabilities and situational factors. Troops often have different POA in the different phases: Assault Phase, Firing Phase and Combat Phase. For more details see the *Combat Mechanism* and the *Firing Mechanism* sections.

Rear Support: A unit can claim rear support if it has a unit of *Steady* or *Disordered* friendly *non-Skirmishers* to its rear. A large unit can claim rear support for itself if it is placed in 'deep' formation. See the *Combat Mechanism* section for details.

Reformed Infantry: Reformed Infantry regiments are mostly assumed to have introduced light infantry companies into their battalion formations and to have stopped using the line as their normal formation during a battle. They move faster in Tactical formation, but slower in line formation than unreformed infantry. Because they have light companies integral to their formation they receive more dice when firing at medium range.

Reforming: Infantry may change their facing to any direction with turning or wheeling as long as they end their formation change no nearer the enemy, and with their centre point as close as possible to its starting position. This takes a full single move.

Regular: Any unit defined as *Conscript*, *Drilled* or *Veteran*.

Reserves: A reserve is a division that is left off-table to the rear of the army and is attempting to enter from a specified sector of the active player's base edge of the table.

Rifles: A unit of Infantry equipped with rifles, or with a rifle attachment has a better chance of causing a casualty on a general. Additionally it only loses 1 dice instead of the normal 2 if firing at medium range and enemy cavalry are within 6MU.

Rockets: Rockets are available to British troops only as attachments to another Artillery unit. They can only fire at long range

Sector (of the table): A table is split into 6 equal sectors, 3 in each players half of the table. Each half of the table has 2 flank sectors (right and left) and a single centre sector. Sectors are used for terrain placement and also for defining the arrival position of a flank march or a reserve force.

Self-supported: A large unit of either Infantry or Cavalry formed up 2 bases wide and 3 bases deep provides rear support for itself, even if *Wavering* or in contact with enemy. A unit in self-supported formation is also considered to be in Tactical formation.

Shock Cavalry: Any Cavalry defined in the army lists as '*shock*'. These will normally be the largest and heaviest men and horses. Examples are: Cuirassiers, Mounted Grenadiers, Carabiniers, etc.

Single Rank: Cavalry and Infantry are considered to be in 'single rank' for the purpose of evading or being shot at if their unit is entirely in a single rank of bases. This represents a formation in which the individual squadrons or battalions within the unit are formed into separate lines 2 or 3 ranks deep, mostly positioned adjacent to each other, but may also be deployed in echelon. The physical depth of the base represents enough distance on the table for this to be possible. Note that two units each 1 base deep but behind each other still count as 1 base deep for the purpose of evading or being shot at.

Skirmishers:

All of the following are considered to be *Skirmishers*:

- Units of Infantry entirely in *Skirmish* formation.
- All units of *Irregular* light Cavalry
- Units of *Regular* light Cavalry deployed in single rank (Extended Line).

Soft Ground: Before the game start any area of the table may be marked and defined as Soft Ground. This would often be used in a scenario or historical game when there is, or has been, a period of heavy rain, or if an area is naturally boggy. This option is not used in points-based games.

Square: A defensive formation used by Infantry when threatened by enemy Cavalry. It is depicted by placing the Infantry unit in Tactical formation with the rear rank facing backwards. A Square has no flank. It has advantages if assaulted by Cavalry and disadvantages when fired upon or if assaulted by Infantry.

***Steady*:** Any unit that is has no cohesion loss markers. A unit can still be *Steady* if it is *Spent*, or is in rough or difficult terrain.

Support Area: The area in which a unit can supply supporting dice to aid the firing of an adjacent unit. See the *Firing Mechanism.*

Supporting unit:

A Unit can only provide support for another unit if it is:

- *Non-Skirmishing* Infantry - if the unit to be supported is Infantry or Artillery.
- Cavalry - if the unit to be supported is Cavalry.
- *Steady* or *Disordered.*
- *Average* or *Superior* if the supported unit is *Superior* or *Guard.*

Tactical Formation: A formation of Infantry or Cavalry, 2 or 3 bases wide and 2 or 3 bases deep with all bases facing in the same direction. A unit of Artillery is also considered to be in Tactical formation when unlimbered unless it is currently abandoned.

Terrain Sizes:

Small: Each must be so sized and shaped that both of the following apply:

- A 4 x 6 MU rectangle can be fitted entirely within its footprint.
- Its entire footprint can be fitted within a 12 MU diameter circle.

Large: Each must be so sized and shaped that all of the following apply:

- A 4 x 6 MU rectangle can be fitted entirely within its footprint.
- Its footprint cannot be entirely fitted within a 12 MU diameter circle.
- Its entire footprint can be fitted within a 16 MU diameter circle.

Unreformed Infantry: Unreformed regiments are mostly assumed to still use the line as their normal formation during a battle. They have no integral *light infantry* companies and because of this they do not receive any firing dice at medium (Skirmisher) range.

Uphill: Unless a hill has clearly defined peaks or ridge crests, it is considered to have a single peak at the most central point of the terrain piece. A single base is uphill if it is has at least 3 of its corners on a hill and the nearest peak or point on a ridge crest is behind a straight line extending its front edge. If bases of both players have their front edge touching a peak or ridge crest, or if both would count uphill using the above definition, then neither counts as uphill. A unit is considered to be uphill if all of its bases in contact are uphill of all enemy bases in contact. It counts as partially uphill if at least one, but not all, its bases count as uphill and none of the enemy bases count as uphill.

Wheel: A move, or partial move, in which one corner of the moving unit remains stationary. This corner will be a front corner if the wheel is forwards and a rear corner if the wheel is backwards.

With: A Commander is with a unit if he is in edge contact with it. He can only be with one unit at a time, and this must be defined by the player if it is not clear. A commander that is with a unit is also considered to be **leading** it.

Within: At or closer than.

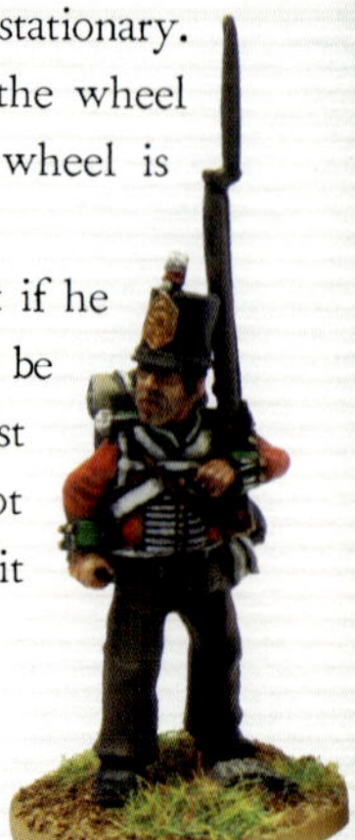

British Infantryman

USING THESE RULES FOR HISTORICAL BATTLES

Refighting *an historical battle* can be both fun and exciting. Many Napoleonic wargamers enjoying the challenge of testing themselves against their historical counterparts, and these rules have been designed to allow this to happen.

The usual rules for the creation of Divisions will of course be discarded, with the actual Orders of Battle (OOB) being used to create an historical organisation for the army. When converting an historical OOB to tabletop *Field of Glory Napoleonic* units it is recommended that players start at the brigade level. As a rule of thumb when converting historical infantry brigades into units, use the following table:

1,200–2,000 men	1 small unit
2,000–3,000 men	1 large unit
3,000–4,000 men	2 small units
4,000–5,000 men	1 small + 1 large unit
5,000 or more	2 large units or 3 small units

When converting historical cavalry brigades into units, use the following table:

500–800 men	1 small unit
800–1,200 men	1 large unit
1,200–1,500 men	2 small units
1,500–1,800 men	1 small + 1 large unit
1,800 or more	2 large units or 3 small units

When converting historical artillery brigades into units, use the following table:

12–19 guns	1 small unit
20–30 guns	1 large unit

If precise conversions are required, players should use a figure scale of 1:55 for Infantry and Cavalry and 1:8 for Artillery.

In most cases a single unit will be equivalent to a single regiment of infantry or several grouped battalions. With many historical Orders of Battle it may be required to split a very large regiment into 2 or more units, or to combine 2 or more small regiments to make a single unit. Of course there are the armies who do not use regiments (or the battalions of a regiment do not fight together in the field). It may also be necessary for a single unit to represent a combination of under strength formations which are differently armed. For example, 2 small light Cavalry regiments may be combined into a single unit of half Uhlans and half Hussars (2 bases of each). The units created can then be placed into their Divisional and Corps commands to match the historical formations.

When converting historical orders of battle for use with these rules players should try to maintain a ratio of not less than 3 units for each *Division Commander*. A higher ratio is acceptable, but if the ratio is less than this players should consider combining 2 small divisions into 1 larger command, and attaching a Brigade Commander to one of the units to compensate.

Large and Grand Batteries of Artillery can be created by combining multiple units under the command of their own *Division Commander*. Normally these would only be used by the main combatants of Austria, France and Russia. But if historical OOBs indicate otherwise, players should feel free to organise them as they wish.

Command and Control is used in much the same way as in a corps level game except that there will be the addition of a higher level *Army Commander*. An *Army Commander* is treated in the same way as a *Corp Commander*, except that he may never join or lead a unit. He suffers the same penalties as does a *Corps Commander* if he moves. He will still be defined as Competent, Skilled and Exceptional with *Command Points* of 1, 2 and 3 respectively. However his Command Range will be double that of a Corps Commander (40MU). At the start of the *Command Point Allocation Phase* he will be allowed to distribute his *Command Points* to his subordinate *Corps Commanders*, after which the *Corps Commanders* can redistribute them to their *Division Commanders* as normal. The *Army Commander* cannot be killed or otherwise become a casualty.

French standard bearer

USING FIGURES BASED FOR OTHER RULE SETS

Some *other rules sets* use the same bases as those suggested for these rules, but most do not. To make it easier to use these rules with those figures we provide the following options:

INFANTRY BASES

Some Infantry bases can be combined to create 8 figure bases compatible with these rules. For example: 2 bases of 4 figures, each 4 wide and 1 deep, or each 2 wide and 2deep, can easily be paired together to make a single base 4 wide and 2 deep.

Where compatible 8 figure bases cannot be created we can instead create compatible units. These can be created by combining multiple bases to form a unit which is as close as possible to the size of standard units. For example, 3 and 6 figure bases can be combined to form a unit whose tactical unit is 3 bases (9 figures) wide and 2 bases (4 figures) deep.

In each case the area occupied by the 'unit' is as close as possible to the area occupied by an equivalent sized unit or standard base sizes. It should be possible to create units of approximately the correct size by combining most bases in this way, with Cavalry and Artillery being treated in the same manner. If non-standard bases as used in this way it should be remembered that the measuring unit '1 base width' will not change. (It will remain 60mm/40mm/30mm). Using this method of forming units, it is possible to play a game with figures based differently on each side, or even in the same army.

One additional rule will be required if different sized bases are being used in the same game. This rule is as follows:

- No player may gain an advantage purely because his figures are based differently to the rules standard.

All other rules apply as normal.

DESIGN PHILOSOPHY

This section explains the rationale behind the different terms used and outlines the design concepts and approaches that we have adopted.

Each member of the *Field of Glory Napoleonic* design team has a keen interest in the history of the Napoleonic wars and between them have amassed over 80 years of wargaming experience. In this rulebook, you take the role of an *Army* or *Corps Commander* and his senior generals, giving the rules a 'from the top down' style and feel. Historical accounts describe battles as a series of events and phases, rather than solely an account of constant action. With *Field of Glory Napoleonic*, we have also tried to reflect this ebb and flow of events on the battlefield.

Napoleonic armies of this era had a common theme, whatever their organisation at the macro level. Each had an overall commander and a few senior commanders who would take control of a corps, a division, brigade, or a sometimes just a group of regiments with orders to fulfil a particular function. Subordinate to these was another layer of commanders who controlled the various Tactical 'formations' which generally consisted of a number of infantry 'battalions' or cavalry 'squadrons' grouped together.

These 'formations' would often be formed from a single regiment (comprising between 2 and 5 battalions, or between 4 and 10 squadrons and 2 or more batteries of artillery). For example, the Coldstream Guards had several battalions in its organisation as did the 95th Rifles. Regiments in many continental armies did operate and manoeuvre together as a Tactical formation on the battlefield. In the earlier part of the period in the French army these were called Demi-brigades. Later and in other armies 'regiments' or plain 'brigades' were used and in turn grouped into Divisions.

But the terminology used varied between nations as did their organisational practices. A Prussian brigade of 1813-1815 was more like an all arms division in other armies and the Prussian army of 1806–1807 and the Austrian army sometimes referred to and used 'columns' meaning a group of units, again of all arms, under a single general officer.

One of Napoleon's most significant contributions to army organisation was the creation of the 'Corps d'Armée'. This was a field force of all arms, typically 25,000 men. It was able to hold its own in an encounter battle with a larger enemy force until other Corps d'Armée could march to the sound of the guns, or under the direction of the Emperor, and join in the battle.

Polish Voltigeur

WHY REGIMENTS AND NOT BATTALIONS OR BRIGADES?

Fixing the Infantry units and their sizing is the essential primary element of this period and around that the other arms Cavalry and Artillery must flow. Many existing and traditional rule sets use battalions and brigades. The first can lead to very detailed games which can be an impediment to big battles (if every battalion is to be represented) and make it hard to get to reasonably quick outcomes, although they are a lot of fun in their own right. Brigade level games may also be much less satisfying visually and aesthetically for those who like to see masses of figures and variety of uniforms and types, which we do.

We have opted for the regiment of several battalions or 'demi-brigade', not just as a compromise for game design reasons and 'the look and feel' but because there is also a good historical foundation for that approach.

Melee in Fuentes de Oñoro, by Patrice Courcelle © Osprey Publishing Ltd.
Taken from Campaign 99: Fuentes de Oñoro 1811

In many published orders of battle available today for the era you will find frequent references to a particular Infantry regiment being present such '73rd Regt du Ligne (3)' and the number in brackets shows how many battalions of that regiment were in that higher level formation. The French could have as many as 6 battalions in a regiment – though seldom all of them present together. This is true in all the major combatants – except for the British.

In those armies where this was standard practice the component battalions would march, train and manoeuvre together and would not usually be split apart on the battlefield though individual battalions might be detached beforehand for other duties, e.g. as garrisons The commanding officers of the battalions (sometimes majors, sometimes colonels) would work together under the senior battalion commander.

Austrian Grenzer

In the 1790s the French revolutionary forces created 'demi-brigades' of three battalions often with one ex-royalist regular battalion in white uniforms ('les blancs') and two of volunteers or *Conscript* levies in blue ('les bleus'). In the Grande Armée Napoleon decided to award eagles only to the first battalion of a regiment, the rest having coloured flags and not tricolours. This was the norm in fact.

It also applies to some of the foreign infantry formations attached to the armies, all of whose constituent battalions would usually operate together. Examples are the Vistula Legion, the Portuguese Legion and the King's German Legion. It also includes small contingents like the Brunswick and Nassau elements in Wellington's 1815 army, and Lützow's Freikorps.

An infantry brigade as defined by the major combatants is therefore too broad a spectrum. British brigades were small – about the size of continental regiments. For example, there were 2 battalions in each of the British Guards brigades at Waterloo. But Prussian ones from 1813 were divisions in size with up to 9 battalions and attached artillery and cavalry.

Using the regiment as the building block is therefore a very flexible way of enabling historical orders of battle to be represented in a reasonably consistent manner.

In a standard game of *Field of Glory Napoleonic* you will take command of an army which consists of approximately 12-18 units led by the *Corps Commander* and his *Division Commanders*. This approximates to a Corps. The game has been designed to ensure that, just as in reality, the commanders (you) are fully occupied with decision making from the outset. Your key objective is to outmanoeuvre the enemy army and concentrate your forces at critical points in the battle – to demonstrate your mastery of what is sometimes referred to as 'Grand Tactics'. This will then destroy the enemy's will to fight, deal a devastating blow to the morale of their commanders (your opponent) and allow you to win. Our companion army list books contain historical overviews and accurately researched information on the organisation of the armies of the period, ensuring that your battles will be able to have a realistic and historical feel.

Although some armies did not take part in the campaigns covered by the period of the army lists, we have included lists for some of the armies, so that you may use them in 'what if' scenarios and for campaign battles. *Field of Glory Napoleonic* will allow you to use any of the forces on the tabletop, using a points system, allowing each army to be scaled up or down whilst retaining an individual mix and balance of troops to create 'what if' encounters.

We started with a blank sheet of paper and looked at a wide range of possible mechanisms. Some concepts are entirely new. Others may look familiar at first glance, but interact with the rest of the rules in a completely new way, giving *Field of Glory Napoleonic* a style all its own. In *Field of Glory Napoleonic* our most important objective is to make the game fun to play whilst retaining a strong historical feel. So whether you fancy being Napoleon, Wellington or the Archduke Charles, it's entirely up to you.

Portuguese Cacadores Officer

APPENDIX 1 – ARMY LISTS

THE ANGLO-PORTUGUESE ARMY OF 1810–1811

This is the army that Wellington and Beresford forged and trained. It had made successful forays into Spain but was still without a decisive victory. The period was one of great contestability between the Allied and French armies in Spain with the allies still not having it all their own way. Wellington's battles tended to still be on the defensive.

The period included some of Wellington's victories including Busaco in Sept 1810 and the Pyrric victory of Albuera. It also included the battle at Fuentes de Onoro after which Wellington commented 'If Boney had been there we should have been beaten'. This serves to show that the two main contending armies had not much to choose between them when it came to the field of battle.

CUSTOMIZED ARMY

Choose an army based on the maxima and minima in the list below. The following special instructions apply to this army:

- All British, Portuguese and KGL infantry move as **Unreformed,** but fire as **Reformed.** They are paid for as **Reformed.**
- All Spanish infantry are **Unreformed.**
- Mixed divisions may not be used.
- Portuguese infantry units must be in divisions that include at least an equal number of British infantry units. A large unit of Portuguese infantry must include an attached officer.
- Portuguese artillery may only be used in a division which contains at least one Portuguese unit.
- A single British Light Division may be used. British light division infantry may only be used in this division. This division may include other British, Portuguese or KGL light infantry and may also include a single British line infantry unit. It cannot include an artillery unit but may include artillery attachments. Rifle units in the division may only be used in skirmish order unless occupying buildings.
- A single infantry or mixed division of Spanish Allies may be included.
- Attachments for the Spanish division must be allocated to units when the army is first created.
- Non-Spanish attachments should be allocated to units after terrain has been placed but before any units have been placed on the table.

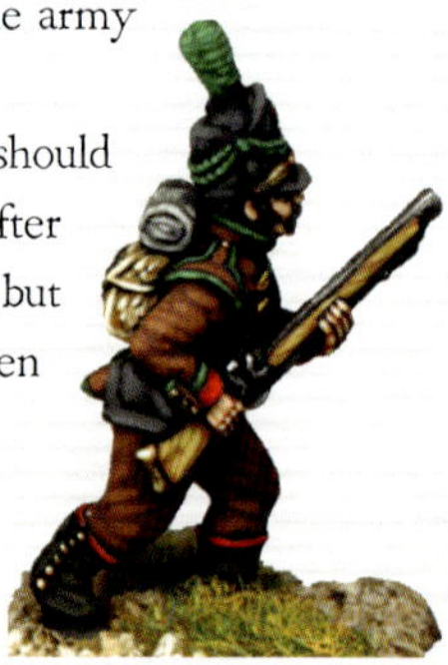

Portuguese Cacadore

ANGLO-PORTUGUESE ARMY 1810–1811 (WELLINGTON)

Territory Types: Spain & Portugal

Initiative Level 1

Commanders

Command Level	Quality	Points per General	Minimum	Maximum	
Corps Commander	Exceptional	80	1		
	Skilled	50			
	Competent	30			
Divisional Commander	Exceptional	80	2	1	4
	Skilled	50		3	
	Competent	30		3	
Charismatic Commander		10	0	1	

Unit Name	Troop Type	Élan	Training	Special Capabilities	Points per base	Bases per unit	Minimum bases	Maximum bases	
Core Infantry									
British Infantry	Line Infantry	Average	Veteran	-	13	4 or 6	8	30	36
			Drilled	-	10		8	12	
British Light Infantry	Light Infantry	Average	Veteran	-	16	4 or 6	4	8	12
				Rifles	17			6	
Kings German Legion (KGL)	Line Infantry	Superior	Veteran	-	17	4	4	10	12
		Average	Veteran	-	13	4 or 6			
KGL Light Infantry	Light Infantry	Average	Veteran	Rifles	17	4		4	
British foot artillery	Medium artillery	Average	Veteran	-	28	2	2	4	
			Drilled		20				
Portuguese foot artillery	Medium artillery	Average	Drilled	-	20		0		
Core Cavalry									
British Dragoon Guards	Heavy Cavalry	Superior	Drilled	Shock, Guard	21	4	0	4	8
British Dragoons	Heavy Cavalry	Average	Drilled	Shock, Impetuous	12	4	4	8	
		Average	Drilled	-	10			4	
KGL Dragoons	Heavy Cavalry	Average	Veteran	Shock	16	4	0	4	
British Hussars	Light Cavalry	Superior	Drilled	-	11	4	0	4	12
British Light Dragoons	Light Cavalry	Average	Drilled	-	8	4	4	4	
				Impetuous	7	4 or 6		8	
KGL Hussars & Light Dragoons	Light Cavalry	Average	Veteran	-	10	4 or 6		6	
Optional Units									
British Foot Guards	Line Infantry	Superior	Veteran	Guards	21	4 or 6	0	6	
Highlanders	Line Infantry	Superior	Veteran	-	17	4 or 6	0	6	
British Light Division Infantry	Light Infantry	Superior	Veteran	Rifles	22	4	0	4	8
				-	21			8	
British Horse artillery	Medium artillery	Average	Veteran	-	32	2	0	2	
			Drilled	-	24				
Portuguese Infantry	Line Infantry	Average	Veteran	-	13	4 or 6	0	4	10
			Drilled		10			8	
Portuguese Cacadores	Light Infantry	Average	Drilled	Rifles	13	4	0	8	
Portuguese Dragoons	Light Cavalry	Average	Drilled	-	8	4 or 6	0	6	

<table>
<tr><th colspan="6">Attachments</th></tr>
<tr><th>Type</th><th>Restrictions</th><th>Special Capabilities</th><th>Points per base</th><th>Minimum bases</th><th>Maximum bases</th></tr>
<tr><td rowspan="2">Skirmishers</td><td rowspan="2">Minimum of 1 and maximum of 3 per infantry division</td><td>-</td><td>8</td><td rowspan="2">1 per division</td><td rowspan="2">3 per division</td></tr>
<tr><td>Rifles</td><td>10</td></tr>
<tr><td>Officers</td><td>No more than 1 per division, attached to an infantry or cavalry unit.</td><td>-</td><td>12</td><td>0</td><td>1 per division</td></tr>
<tr><td rowspan="2">Artillery</td><td rowspan="2">Up to 3, plus up to 1 attachment of Rockets to a foot artillery unit.</td><td>Medium</td><td>10</td><td>0</td><td>3 (+1)</td></tr>
<tr><td>Rockets</td><td>12</td><td>0</td><td>1</td></tr>
<tr><td>Cavalry</td><td colspan="5">None allowed</td></tr>
</table>

<table>
<tr><th colspan="10">SPANISH ALLIES</th></tr>
<tr><th>Command Level</th><th colspan="4">Quality</th><th colspan="2">Points per General</th><th>Minimum</th><th colspan="2">Maximum</th></tr>
<tr><td rowspan="2">Division Commander</td><td colspan="4">Skilled</td><td colspan="2">40</td><td rowspan="2">0</td><td colspan="2" rowspan="2">1</td></tr>
<tr><td colspan="4">Competent</td><td colspan="2">20</td></tr>
<tr><th>Unit Name</th><th>Troop Type</th><th>Elan</th><th>Training</th><th>Special Capabilities</th><th>Points per base</th><th>Bases per unit</th><th>Minimum bases</th><th colspan="2">Maximum bases</th></tr>
<tr><th colspan="10">Core Troops</th></tr>
<tr><td>Spanish & Walloon Guards</td><td>Line Infantry</td><td>Average</td><td>Drilled</td><td>Guard</td><td>12</td><td>4 or 6</td><td>0</td><td colspan="2">6</td></tr>
<tr><td rowspan="2">Spanish Infantry</td><td rowspan="2">Line Infantry</td><td>Average</td><td rowspan="2">Drilled</td><td rowspan="2">-</td><td>8</td><td rowspan="2">4</td><td rowspan="2">8</td><td>4</td><td rowspan="2">12</td></tr>
<tr><td>Poor</td><td>6</td><td>12</td></tr>
<tr><td>Spanish Field artillery</td><td>Medium Artillery</td><td>Poor</td><td>Drilled</td><td>-</td><td>16</td><td>2</td><td>0</td><td colspan="2">2</td></tr>
<tr><td rowspan="2">Spanish Dragoons</td><td rowspan="2">Heavy Cavalry</td><td>Average</td><td rowspan="2">Drilled</td><td rowspan="2">-</td><td>10</td><td rowspan="2">4</td><td rowspan="2">0</td><td>4</td><td rowspan="2">8</td></tr>
<tr><td>Poor</td><td>8</td><td>8</td></tr>
<tr><th colspan="10">Attachments</th></tr>
<tr><th>Type</th><th colspan="4">Restrictions</th><th>Special Capabilities</th><th>Points per base</th><th>Minimum bases</th><th colspan="2">Maximum bases</th></tr>
<tr><td>Skirmishers</td><td colspan="4">Up to 1 allowed</td><td>Rifles</td><td>10</td><td>0</td><td colspan="2">1</td></tr>
<tr><td>Officers</td><td colspan="5">None allowed</td><td>12</td><td>0</td><td colspan="2">0</td></tr>
<tr><td>Artillery</td><td colspan="5">up to 1 allowed</td><td>10</td><td>0</td><td colspan="2">1</td></tr>
<tr><td>Cavalry</td><td colspan="5">up to 1 allowed if no cavalry purchased</td><td>6</td><td>0</td><td colspan="2">1</td></tr>
</table>

THE SPANISH ARMY OF 1810–1812

The regular Spanish army of this time was generally viewed as poorly trained, badly equipped, under strength, and badly led. This reputation may be an exaggeration but there is some considerable truth behind it. Wellington held its officer Corps in very low esteem, although French generals had a higher opinion of the rank and file. It should also be noted that the French had more regular soldiers in the theatre than the Spanish for most of the period. It did however, from to time, perform extremely well, as at Baylen, Tarnames, Alcaniz and San Marcial. From the start the Spanish army numbered over 100,000 men and by 1812 had some 160,000 – more than the Anglo Portuguese armies combined and more than any other nation save the great powers of Europe.

At the start of the war, and for most of it, the regular army of Spain was of variable, often poor quality with mostly under-strength units especially of cavalry. Field Artillery units came in all shapes and sizes with no standard gun types. The army also contained substantial numbers of militia and foreign regiments rather like the army of Bourbon France. On rare occasions during the war guerrilla bands would join the regular army in field actions. Despite several changes of governmental structure the organisation of the army changed little throughout. By 1810 the initial surge of volunteers had waned, some experience gained, and average quality was beginning to creep up. The odd capable general was emerging and there was less dependence on militia and volunteers.

CUSTOMIZED ARMY

Choose an army based on the maxima and minima in the list below. The following special instructions apply to this army:

- Infantry units are **Unreformed.**
- Any number of Mixed Divisions may be used.
- Attachments must be allocated to units when the army is first created.

Spanish Guerillas

THE ARMY OF SPAIN 1810–1812									
Territory Types: Spain & Portugal									
Initiative Level 1									
Commanders									
Command Level	**Quality**				**Points per General**		**Minimum**	**Maximum**	
Corps Commanders	Skilled				50		1		
	Competent				30				
Division Commander	Exceptional				80		1	1	4
	Skilled				50		2	2	
	Competent				30			4	
Unit Name	**Troop Type**	**Elan**	**Training**	**Special Capabilities**	**Points per base**	**Bases per unit**	**Minimum bases**	**Maximum bases**	
Core Infantry									
Regular Infantry	Line Infantry	Average	Drilled	-	8	4-6	4	8	32
		Poor	Drilled		6		8	16	
		Average	Conscript		6		4	16	
Cazadores & Tiradores	Light Infantry	Average	Veteran	-	16	4	4	4	8
			Drilled		12			8	
Militia	Line Infantry	Average	Conscript	-	6	4	4	16	
Field Artilery	Medium Artillery	Average	Drilled	-	20	2	2		

Core Cavalry									
Heavy Dragoons	Heavy Cavalry	Average	Drilled	-	10	4	4	4	12
		Poor	Drilled	-	8				
Light Dragoons	Light Cavalry	Poor	Drilled	-	7	4		8	
Line cavalry	Heavy Cavalry	Average	Drilled	shock	13	4		4	
Optional Units									
Spanish Guards	Guard Infantry	Average	Drilled	Guard	12	4	0	4	8
Grenadiers	Line Infantry	Average	Veteran	-	10	4	0	8	
Guerrillas	Light Infantry	Average	Irregulars	-	8	4 or 6	0	8	
Dismounted Dragoons	Line Infantry	Poor	Drilled	-	6	4	0	4	
Volunteers	Line Infantry	Average	Conscript	-	6	4 or 6	0	10	
Hussars & Cazadores	Light Cavalry	Poor	Drilled	-	6	4	0	4	4
Lancers	Light Cavalry	Poor	Drilled	Lance	8	4	0	4	
4 pdr Horse Artillery	Horse Artillery	Average	Drilled	-	24	2	0	2	

Attachments

Type	Restrictions	Points per base	Minimum bases	Maximum bases
Skirmishers	Up to 1 skirmisher attachment may be purchased for each 3 regular infantry units.	8	0	1 per 3 regular units
Officers	No more than 1	12	0	1
Artillery	Up to 1 medium attachment in a division with no artillery unit	10	0	1 per division
Cavalry	Up to 1 allowed per infantry division	6	0	1 per infantry division

FRENCH INFANTRY CORPS D'ARMÉE 1812

The French Corps d'Armée in Russia, however well equipped and organised, was by now substantively leavened by conscription, with time and the impact of the war in Spain drawing off veteran officers, NCOs, and men as well as material. Despite the death toll of leaders in 1809, it still contained many outstanding commanders at Divisional level, for example Generals Friant, Gudin and Morand. Perhaps the best run and led Corps was Davout's First Corps which had 60,000 men at the start of 1812. Organised into 5 Divisions it was larger than many armies in the earlier years of the wars. French Corps d'Armée often contained many non French regiments – for example Swiss, Portuguese and Croatians – which were part of the established French national army rather than national contingents from other nations. We have included in this list the option of fielding one or more allied divisions under the command of a French Corps Commander. Not included in this list is the Imperial Guard, which by this period was virtually an army all on its own.

French Voltigeur

CUSTOMIZED ARMY

Choose an army based on the maxima and minima in the list below. The following special instructions apply to this army:

- Infantry units are **Reformed.**
- At least one French infantry division must be used.
- Up to 2 mixed divisions may be used. Only 1 of these may be French. Mixed divisions may only contain core cavalry units, up to a maximum of 2.
- Infantry from the *Allied Contingents* list may not be used in divisions containing any French, but may be combined in infantry or mixed divisions with other allied contingents. Their commander will be classified as allied.
- Cavalry from the *Allied Contingents* list may be used in their own mixed or cavalry division with an appropriate allied commander. They may also be used in a cavalry division under a French commander if at least half the cavalry units in it are French.
- The minima for allied troops are ignored if no allied troops are used. If allied troops are used the number of bases used count towards the minima for French troops in the main list.
- Any French foot artillery unit may have an attachment of either howitzers or heavy artillery, up to a maximum 1 of each.
- French artillery units may have an officer attachment.
- Attachments must be allocated as follows:
  - Attachments must be allocated to units in non-French allied divisions when the army is first created.
  - Attachments are allocated to French divisions when purchased, but only allocated to units after terrain placement and immediately before deployment.

FRENCH INFANTRY CORPS D'ARMEE 1812

Territory Types:	Central Europe, Eastern Europe
Initiative:	3

Commanders

Command Level	Quality	Points per General	Minimum	Maximum	
Corps Commanders	Exceptional	80	1		
	Skilled	50			
	Competent	30			
Divisional Commander	Exceptional	80	2	2	4
	Skilled	50		2	
	Competent	30		3	
Charismatic Commander		+ 10	0	1	

Unit Name	Troop Type	Elan	Training	Special Capabilities	Points per base	Bases per unit	Minimum bases	Maximum bases	
Core Infantry									
French Line Infantry	Line Infantry	Average	Veteran	-	13	4	10	12	50
			Drilled		10	4 or 6		18	
			Conscript		7		8	30	
French Light Infantry	Light Infantry	Average	Veteran	-	16	4	4	8	12
			Drilled		12	4 or 6		12	
6 or 8 pdr Field Artillery	Medium artillery	Average	Veteran	-	28	2 or 3	4	6	7
			Drilled		20				
12 pdr Field Artillery	Heavy artillery	Average	Veteran	-	32	2	0	3	
			Drilled		24	2 or 3			
Core Cavalry									
Hussars	Light Cavalry	Superior	Drilled	-	11	4	4	8	16
		Average			8	4 or 6			
Chasseurs a Cheval	Light Cavalry	Superior	Drilled	-	11	4	4	14	
		Average			8	4 or 6			
6 pdr Horse Artillery	Horse Artillery	Average	Veteran	-	32	2	0	2	
			Drilled		24				
Optional Units									
Swiss Line Infantry	Line Infantry	Superior	Drilled	-	14	4	0	8	16
		Average	Veteran		13				
Croatian Line Infantry	Line Infantry	Average	Drilled	-	10	4	0	8	
Portuguese Legion	Line Infantry	Average	Drilled	-	10	4 or 6	0	8	
Cuirassiers	Heavy Cavalry	Average	Veteran	Shock	16	4	0	8	12
			Drilled		13	4 or 6			
Dragoons	Heavy Cavalry	Average	Veteran	-	13	4	0	8	
			Drilled		10	4 or 6			
Polish Uhlans	Light Cavalry	Average	Veteran	Lances	12	4	0	4	

Attachments

Type	Restrictions	Special Capabilities	Points per base	Minimum bases	Maximum bases
Skirmishers	Up to 1 per division for French units only		8	0	1 per division
Officers	Up to 1 per division		12	0	1 per division
Artillery	Up to 1 per division for French units only	Medium	10	0	1 per division
		Heavy	12	0	
		Howitzer	12	0	
Cavalry	Up to 2 per non-mixed division for French units only.		6	0	1 per division

ALLIED CONTINGENTS

Commanders

Command Level	Quality	Points per General	Minimum	Maximum	
Divisional Commander	Skilled	40	1	1	2
	Competent	20		2	

Unit Name	Troop Type	Elan	Training	Special Capabilities	Points per base	Bases per unit	Minimum bases	Maximum bases	
Core Infantry									
Berg Infantry	Line Infantry	Average	Drilled	-	10	4	12	8	30
			Conscript		8				
Baden Line Infantry	Line Infantry	Average	Drilled	-	10	4 or 6		8	
Hessian Guard infantry	Guard Infantry	Average	veteran	Guard	17	4		4	
Saxon Infantry	Line Infantry	Average	Conscript	-	8	4		8	
Polish Infantry	Line Infantry	Superior	Drilled	-	14	4		8	
		Average			10	4 or 6			
Neapolitan Infantry	Line Infantry	Poor	Conscript	-	4	4 or 6		12	
Rhienbund Infantry	Line Infantry	Average	Conscript	-	6	4 or 6		12	
Allied 6 or 8 pdr Field Artillery	Medium Artillery	Average	Drilled	-	20	2 or 3	0	4	
Core Cavalry									
Neapolitan Velites a Cheval	Light Cavalry	Poor	Drilled	-	7	4	8	4	
Neapolitan Gardes d'Honneur	Light Cavalry	Poor	Drilled	Guards	11	4		4	
Baden Hussars	Light Cavalry	Superior	Veteran	-	13	4		4	
Hessian& Saxon Cheveauleger	Light Cavalry	Superior	Veteran	-	13	4 or 6		6	
Lancers de Berg	Light Cavalry	Superior	Veteran	Lances	15	4		4	

Attachments

Type	Restrictions	Points per base	Minimum bases	Maximum bases
Skirmishers	No more than 1 of each per division	8	0	1 per division
Officers		12	0	1 per division
Artillery		10	0	1 per division
Cavalry	None allowed			

THE RUSSIAN ARMY OF 1812

The composition of the Russian army by 1812 was flexible but based around a core mix of line musketeers and Jaegers in infantry formations always with a strong foundation of medium and heavy artillery. The full range of line cavalry could be part of the Corps order of battle or pulled out into reserves.

The Russian Guard, which by now was as substantial as the French, was formed into a single Corps at Borodino with some line units in addition but could be made part of other Corps formations at need. It had all arms of the service represented. Like the French it had a 'Young' Guard but, unlike the French equivalent, it was formed from elite and veteran line units mainly ex-Grenadiers. The lists allow for these various types of formation. The Opolochenie were poorly armed militia, often armed with pikes due to a lack of muskets.

CUSTOMIZED ARMY

Choose an army based on the maxima and minima in the list below. The following special instructions apply to this army:

- Russian infantry are **Reformed.**
- Foot guards, shock cavalry and Opolchenie may not be in the same division as each other.
- If used, guard infantry must all be in the same infantry division, which may only additionally contain grenadier infantry units and one or both guard artillery units.
- Up to 1 Mixed division may be used, which may not contain any guards or cuirassiers.
- All infantry and mixed divisions MUST contain a minimum of 3 infantry units, and 1 artillery unit.
- Artillery units may have artillery attachments or officer attachments.
- Attachments must all be allocated to units when the army is first created.
- Fieldworks must be deployed after terrain placement and before deployment.

Russian Infantry

RUSSIAN CORPS ARMY OF THE WEST 1812									
Territory Types:	Eastern Europe								
Initiative Level	1								
				Commanders					
Command Level	**Quality**				**Points per General**		**Minimum**	**Maximum**	
Corps Commander	Skilled				50		1		
	Competent				30				
Division Commander	Skilled				50		2	2	3
	Competent				30			3	
Charismatic Commander					+10		0	1	
Unit Name	**Troop Type**	**Elan**	**Training**	**Special Capabilities**	**Points per base**	**Bases per unit**	**Minimum bases**	**Maximum bases**	
				Core Infantry					
Musketeers	Line Infantry	Average	Drilled	-	10	4 or 6	8	48	60
		Average	Conscript	-	7	4 or 6	4	20	
		Poor	Drilled	-	8	4 or 6			
Grenadiers	Line Infantry	Superior	Drilled	-	14	4	0	12	
		Average	Veteran	-	13	4 or 6			
Jaegers	Light Infantry	Average	Veteran	-	16	4	4	4	12
		Average	Drilled	-	12	4 or 6		12	
6pdr Field Artillery	Medium Artillery	Average	Veteran	-	28	2	2	2	8
			Drilled	-	20	2 or 3		6	
12 pdr Field Artillery	Heavy Artillery	Average	Veteran	-	32	2	2	3	
			Drilled	-	24	2 or 3			

Core Cavalry								
Dragoons	Heavy Cavalry	Average	Veteran	-	13	4	8	12
		Average	Drilled	-	10	4 or 6		
Hussars	Light Cavalry	Average	Veteran	-	10	4 or 6		
			Drilled	-	8			
Cossacks	Irregular Cavalry	Average	Irregular	-	7	4 or 6		
6pdr Horse Artillery	Horse Artillery	Average	Veteran	-	32	2	0	3
			Drilled	-	24	2 or 3		
Optional Units								
Foot Guards	Line Infantry	Superior	Drilled	Guard	18	4 or 6	0	12
		Average	Veteran		17			
Guard 6 pdr Artillery	Medium Artillery	Superior	Drilled	Guard	32	2	0	2
Guard 12 pdr Artillery	Heavy Artillery	Superior	Drilled	Guard	36	2	0	2
Uhlans	Light Cavalry	Average	Drilled	-	10	4 or 6	0	6
Cuirassiers	Heavy Cavalry	Average	Veteran	Shock	16	4	0	8
		Average	Drilled		13	4 or 6		
Opolchenie	Line Infantry	Poor	Conscript	-	4	6	0	12
Fieldworks	-	-	-	-	10	2 or 3	0	6

Attachments

Type	Restrictions	Special Capabilities	Points per base	Minimum bases	Maximum bases
Skirmishers	None		8	0	0
Officers	Up to 1 per division		12	0	1 per division
Artillery	Up to 1 per unit in an infantry division, or 1 per 3 units in a cavalry division.	Medium	10	1	1 per infantry unit
		Heavy	12		
Cavalry	Up to 1 per infantry division		6	0	1 per division

THE OTTOMAN TURKISH ARMY OF 1809–1812

This list covers the various armies that fought the Russians and Serbians along the Danube in Wallacia and Bulgaria. The regular troops (Capou-Koulis) of the Ottomans were composed mainly of the Janissaries (infantry) and the Suvarileri (cavalry), each organised into regiments (Ortas). The Orta was the tactical unit and numbered about 2,000 to 3,000 men. In addition to the Capou-Koulis, the Ottoman army contained many regiments raised by the local governors (Pashas) to supplement the regulars as and when needed. The Pasha was expected to provide a specified number of troops at his own expense and often included feudal troops from Albania, Bosnia and other mercenaries to swell the ranks. The Ottoman practice in battle was to fight on the tactical defensive which centred upon a strong defensive line of fieldworks and artillery, with heavy cavalry deployed on the flanks.

CUSTOMIZED ARMY

Choose an army based on the maxima and minima in the list below. The following special instructions apply to this army:

- All infantry are **Unreformed.**
- Up to 1 mixed division may be used. It may contain up to 3 light cavalry units.
- Rayas, if used, must always be in skirmish order.
- Artillery marked as immobile* must always be deployed in fieldworks. They may not be moved.
- At least 1/3 of the non-commander bases in the army must be cavalry.
- An ottoman army may use up to 1 mixed division per corps.
- No allies may be used, not may the Ottomans provide allies to other nations.
- Attachments must be allocated to all units when the army is first created.

<table>
<tr><th colspan="10">OTTOMAN ARMY OF 1809–1812</th></tr>
<tr><td>Territory Types:</td><td colspan="9">Eastern Europe, Southern Europe, Egypt & Middle East</td></tr>
<tr><td>Initiative:</td><td colspan="9">0</td></tr>
<tr><th colspan="10">Commanders</th></tr>
<tr><th>Command Level</th><th colspan="4">Quality</th><th colspan="2">Points per General</th><th>Minimum</th><th colspan="2">Maximum</th></tr>
<tr><td rowspan="2">Corps Commanders</td><td colspan="4">Skilled</td><td>50</td><td>-</td><td colspan="3" rowspan="2">1</td></tr>
<tr><td colspan="4">Competent</td><td>30</td><td>-</td></tr>
<tr><td rowspan="3">Divisional Commander</td><td colspan="4">Exceptional</td><td>80</td><td>-</td><td rowspan="3">2</td><td>1</td><td rowspan="3">4</td></tr>
<tr><td colspan="4">Skilled</td><td>50</td><td>-</td><td>1</td></tr>
<tr><td colspan="4">Competent</td><td>30</td><td>-</td><td>4</td></tr>
<tr><td colspan="5">Charismatic Commander</td><td>+10</td><td>-</td><td>0</td><td colspan="2">1</td></tr>
<tr><th>Unit Name</th><th>Troop Type</th><th>Elan</th><th>Training</th><th>Special Capabilities</th><th>Points per base</th><th>Bases per unit</th><th>Minimum bases</th><th colspan="2">Maximum bases</th></tr>
<tr><th colspan="10">Core Infantry</th></tr>
<tr><td rowspan="3">Janissaries - Benluks</td><td rowspan="2">Line infantry</td><td>Average</td><td>Drilled</td><td rowspan="3">-</td><td>8</td><td rowspan="3">4 or 6</td><td rowspan="3">0</td><td>8</td><td rowspan="5">32</td></tr>
<tr><td>Superior</td><td>Conscripts</td><td>9</td><td>20</td></tr>
<tr><td>Light infantry</td><td>Average</td><td>Drilled</td><td>12</td><td>8</td></tr>
<tr><td rowspan="2">Janissaries - Djemaats</td><td rowspan="2">Line Infantry</td><td>Average</td><td>Conscripts</td><td rowspan="2">-</td><td>6</td><td rowspan="2">4 or 6</td><td rowspan="2">8</td><td>8</td></tr>
<tr><td>Superior</td><td>Irregular</td><td>10</td><td>20</td></tr>
<tr><td>Sekhans - Arnuats</td><td>Light infantry</td><td rowspan="2">Average</td><td>Conscripts</td><td rowspan="2">-</td><td>9</td><td>4 or 6</td><td rowspan="2">8</td><td>12</td><td rowspan="2">20</td></tr>
<tr><td>Other Sekhans</td><td>Light infantry</td><td>Irregular</td><td>8</td><td>4</td><td>12</td></tr>
<tr><td>Fellahin</td><td>Line infantry</td><td>Poor</td><td>Irregular</td><td>-</td><td>5</td><td>6</td><td>6</td><td colspan="2">18</td></tr>
<tr><td rowspan="3">Foot artillery (Topijis)</td><td rowspan="3">Medium foot artillery</td><td>Average</td><td rowspan="3">Drilled</td><td rowspan="3">-</td><td>20</td><td>2</td><td>0</td><td>2</td><td rowspan="3">5</td></tr>
<tr><td rowspan="2">Poor</td><td>16</td><td>2</td><td rowspan="2">2</td><td>2</td></tr>
<tr><td>16</td><td>3</td><td>6</td></tr>
<tr><th colspan="10">Core Cavalry</th></tr>
<tr><td>Suvarileri</td><td>Heavy Cavalry</td><td>Average</td><td>Drilled</td><td>Impetuous, Lancers</td><td>11</td><td>6</td><td>6</td><td>12</td><td rowspan="3">24</td></tr>
<tr><td>Sipahis of the Porte</td><td rowspan="2">Light Cavalry</td><td rowspan="2">Average</td><td>Drilled</td><td>Lancers</td><td>10</td><td>4 or 6</td><td>0</td><td>6</td></tr>
<tr><td>Other Siphais</td><td>Irregular</td><td>Impetuous, Lancers</td><td>8</td><td>6</td><td>8</td><td>18</td></tr>
<tr><td>Yoruks</td><td>Light Cavalry</td><td>Average</td><td>Irregular</td><td>Impetuous</td><td>6</td><td>4 or 6</td><td>4</td><td colspan="2">12</td></tr>
<tr><td>Djellis</td><td>Light Cavalry</td><td>Superior</td><td>Irregular</td><td>Impetuous, Lancers</td><td>11</td><td>4 or 6</td><td>4</td><td colspan="2">12</td></tr>
</table>

Optional Units									
Janissary Bostanci Guard	Line infantry	Average	Drilled	Guard	12	4 or 6	0	8	
Bektasi Dervishes	Line Infantry	Superior	Irregular	Impetuous	9	4	0	4	
Rayas	Light infantry	Average	Veteran	-	16	4	0	4	
Derbents	Line infantry	Average	Conscripts	-	6	4	0	8	12
	Light infantry		Irregular		8	6		12	
Silahtar Guards	Heavy Cavalry	Average	Drilled	Shock, Lancers, Guard	19	4 or 6	0	6	10
Sipahi Oglans		Superior			23			4	
Mamluk Guards	Light Cavalry	Superior	Drilled	Lancers, Guards	17	4	0	4	
Other mixed guard light cavalry	Light Cavalry	Average	Drilled	Lancers, Guards	14	4 or 6	0	6	
Other Mamluks	Heavy Cavalry	Superior	Irregular	Impetuous, Lancers	14	4 or 6	0	6	
Humbaraci (mortars)	Heavy artillery	Superior	Drilled	Immobile*	26	2	0	2	
Provincial artillery	Heavy artillery	Average	Drilled	Immobile*	19	3	0	3	
Fieldworks	-	-	-	-	10	2 or 3	0	5	

Attachments				
Type	**Restrictions**	**Points per base**	**Minimum bases**	**Maximum bases**
Skirmishers	Only janissaries (including Bostanci) may have attachments. These will be of Rayas, with a maximum of 1 per 2 units.	8	0	1 per 2 Janissaries
Officers	No more than 1 per division and a maximum of 2	12	0	2
Artillery	Up to 1 medium artillery attachment to a non-irregular infantry unit.	12	0	1
Cavalry	Suvalleri attachment - up to 2 allowed to non-Arnaut Sekhans	6	0	2

FRENCH INFANTRY CORPS D'ARMÉE 1813

After the summer armistice in 1813 the French army in central Europe was considerably strengthened and reorganised from its weak position in the earlier part of the year following the disaster of the Russian campaign. The proportion of provisional and reserve infantry regiments had reduced by the renewal of hostilities and many had gained battlefield experience .More French Allies began to appear – Danes, Poles, Saxons and the Army of Italy. Cavalry strengths were also up but there remained the issue of quality. With one exception in August 1813 no French Infantry Corps had a cavalry Division, only a weak Brigade, and even that cavalry Division was of brigade strength.

CUSTOMIZED ARMY

Choose an army based on the maxima and minima in the list below. The following special instructions apply to this army:

- Infantry units are **Reformed.**
- Any number of mixed divisions may be used.
- Cavalry, if purchased, MUST be in a mixed division and there may be no more than 2 cavalry units in each with a maximum of 8 stands.
- Cavalry attachments for infantry are only allowed if no cavalry units are purchased.
- No attachments to cavalry units are permitted.

- French naval artillery units and non-French allied units must be in their own separate infantry or mixed division, which cannot contain other French units.
- Artillery attachments may only be purchased if no more than 4 bases of artillery units have been purchased. Heavy artillery attachments can only be added to medium artillery units.
- No more than 2 heavy artillery bases (units or attachments) may be used.
- Attachments must be allocated as follows:
- Attachments must be allocated to units in non-mixed divisions when the army is first created.
- Attachments for mixed divisions must be allocated after terrain placement and immediately before deployment.

FRENCH INFANTRY CORPS D'ARMEE AUGUST 1813

Territory Types:	Central Europe			
Initiative Level	2			
Commanders				
Command Level	**Quality**	**Points per General**	**Minimum**	**Maximum**
Corps Commanders	Exceptional	80	1	
	Skilled	50		
	Competent	30		
Divisional Commander	Exceptional	80	2	1 / 4
	Skilled	50		3
	Competent	30		2
Charismatic Commander		+ 10	0	1

Unit Name	Troop Type	Élan	Training	Special Capabilities	Points per base	Bases per unit	Minimum bases	Maximum bases	
Core Infantry									
French Regular Line Infantry	Line Infantry	Average	Veteran	-	13	4 or 6	0	24	32
			Drilled		10		8		
			Conscript		7		16		
French Reserve and provisional Infantry	Line Infantry	Average	Conscript	-	7	4		24	
		Poor	Conscript		5				
French Regular Light Infantry	Light Infantry	Average	Veteran	-	16	4	4	4	8
			Drilled		12			4	
French provisional Light Infantry	Light Infantry	Average	Conscript	-	9	4		4	
		Poor	Drilled		9				
6 pdr Field Artillery	Medium Atillery	Average	Veteran	-	28	2	4	2	8
			Drilled	-	20			8	
12 pdr Field Artillery	Heavy Artillery	Average	Veteran	-	32	2	0	2	
			Drilled	-	24				
Core Cavalry									
French Chasseurs a Cheval	Light Cavalry	Average	Drilled	-	8	4	4	6	
		Poor			7	4 or 6			
		Average	Conscript		6				
French Hussars	Light Cavalry	Average	Drilled	-	8	4		4	
Optional Troops									
French Naval Artillery and Marine Infantry	Line Infantry	Average	Drilled	-	10	4	0	16	
Irish Legion	Line Infantry	Poor	Conscript		5	4	0	4	
Baden Infantry	Line Infantry	Average	Veteran	-	13	4	0		
			Drilled		10				
Croatian & Dalmatian Infantry	Line Infantry	Average	Veteran	-	13	4	0		
			Drilled		10				

Hesse Darsmtadt Lieb Garde	Guard Infantry	Average	Drilled	Guard	14	4	0	4	8
Hesse Darsmtadt Line Infantry	Line Infantry	Average	Drilled	-	10	4	0	8	
Saxon Infantry	Line Infantry	Poor	Drilled	-	8	4	0	8	
French Dragoons	Heavy Cavalry	Average	Drilled	-	10	4	0	4	8
		Poor			8	4 or 6		8	
Baden Light Dragoons	Light Cavalry	Average	Drilled	-	8	4	0	4	

Attachments						
Type	Restrictions		Special Capabilities	Points per base	Minimum bases	Maximum bases
Skirmisher	Up to 1 skirmisher attachment may be purchased for each 3 line infantry units.		8	1	0	(1 per 3) line
Officers	No more than 1 per division		12	1	0	1 per division
Artillery	Up to 1 per division.	Medium	10	1	0	1 per division
		Heavy	12	1	0	
Cavalry	Up to 1 allowed in a division with no cavalry unit.		6	1	0	1 per division

THE PRUSSIAN ARMY OF 1813

This list can be used to build a Prussian corps of late 1813. By this time the army included large numbers of Landwehr units, which had been rapidly raised and equipped. They formed almost half of all Infantry and Cavalry units in the army. Prussian troops in 1813–1814 were of four types: Regular, Reserve, Landwehr and Volunteers. The volunteers provided many independent jaeger companies, mostly armed with rifles, and were attached to the Regular and Reserve units in the field (but not usually to Landwehr units).

The army was organised into brigades, which were really mixed divisions, each with their own Infantry, Cavalry, and Artillery. Light infantry called *Fusiliers* were assigned in single battalions into the brigades and so are represented by skirmisher attachments (non-rifles).

CUSTOMIZED ARMY

Choose an army based on the maxima and minima in the list below. The following special instructions apply to this army:

- Infantry units are **Reformed.**
- Any number of mixed divisions may be formed. Each mixed division may contain up to 2 dragoon or light cavalry units. More than half the units in each must be infantry.
- Each Infantry and Mixed division must have at least one Landwehr unit.
- Infantry divisions must contain at least one cavalry attachment.
- A single cavalry division may be included, which must contain either dragoons or cuirassiers (not both). The Cavalry division may contain up to 3 heavy cavalry units, plus any number of light cavalry units.
- If used, guards must all be in the same mixed division, which may not contain any non-guards units.
- Artillery units can have attachments of medium artillery or howitzers.
- Attachments must be allocated to their respective divisions when first purchased and to units after terrain placement, but before deployment.

INTRODUCTION
TROOP TYPES
GATHERING YOUR FORCES
ORGANISING YOUR ARMY
PLAYING THE GAME
DETAILED RULES
VICTORY AND DEFEAT
SPECIAL FEATURES
REFERENCE SECTION
POINTS SYSTEM
SETTING UP A POINTS BASED GAME
GLOSSARY OF TERMS
USING THESE RULES FOR HISTORICAL BATTLES
USING FIGURES BASED FOR OTHER RULE SETS
DESIGN PHILOSOPHY
APPENDIX 1 - ARMY LISTS
APPENDIX 2 - HISTORICAL BATTLES
ARTWORK REFERENCES
INDEX

PRUSSIAN ARMY CORPS 1813

Territory Types: Central Europe

Initiative Level 3

Commanders					
Command Level	**Quality**	**Points per General**	**Minimum**	**Maximum**	
Corps Commander	Exceptional	80	1		
	Skilled	50			
	Competent	30			
Divisional Commander	Exceptional	80	2	1	4
	Skilled	50		2	
	Competent	30		3	
Charismatic Commander		10	0	2	

Unit Name	Troop Type	Elan	Training	Special Capabilities	Points per base	Bases per unit	Minimum bases	Maximum bases	
Core Infantry									
Musketeers	Line Infantry	Average	Veteran	-	13	4	0	4	40
			Drilled		10		8	12	
Landwehr	Line Infantry	Superior	Conscript	-	11	4 or 6	0	30	
		Average			7		12		
		Poor			5				
Field Artillery	Medium artillery	Average	Drilled	-	20	2 or 3	2	5	5
	Heavy Artillery	Average	Drilled		24	2	0	2	
Core Cavary									
Dragoons	Heavy cavalry	Average	Drilled	-	10	4 or 6	4	8	8
		Superior			14	4		4	
Hussars	Light cavalry	Average	Drilled	-	8	4	4	4	
Landwehr Cavalry	Light cavalry	Average	Conscript	-	6	4 or 6	6	12	
				Lances	8				
Horse Artillery	Horse Artillery	Average	Drilled	-	24	2	2	2	
Optional units									
Reserve Infantry	Line Infantry	Average	Drilled	-	10	4 or 6	0	16	
		Poor			8				
Guard Infantry	Line Infantry	Average	Veteran	Guard	17	4	0	8	
Leib Infantry	Line Infantry	Average	Veteran	-	13	4 or 6	0		
Uhlans	Light cavalry	Average	Drilled	Lances	10	4	0	4	
Cuirassiers	Heavy Cavalry	Average	Drilled	Shock	13	4 or 6	0	12	14
			Veteran		16			4	
Guard Cuirassiers	Heavy Cavalry	Average	Veteran	Guard, Shock	17	4 or 6	0	6	

Attachments					
Type	**Restrictions**	**Special Capabilities**	**Points per base**	**Minimum bases**	**Maximum bases**
Skirmishers	At least 1 per infantry or mixed division. Maximum of 1 per non-Landwehr unit. At least half of all skirmisher attachments must be rifles.	Muskets	8	1 per Infantry or mixed division	1 per non-landwehr unit
		Rifles	10		
Officers	No more than 1 per division		12	0	1 per division
Artillery	At least 1 per division. Up to 2 in a division with no Artillery unit. 1 Howitzer attachment to an Artillery unit is allowed	Medium	10	1 per division	2 per division
		Howitzers	12		
Cavalry	Minimum of 1 and maximum of 2 per Infantry Division		6	1 per infantry division	2 per Infantry division

THE AUSTRIAN ARMY OF 1813

This list covers the Austrian army of Bohemia from August 1813. After the defeat of 1809 Austria had to limit her army to 150,000 men. During 1812 it had provided a Corps of 30,000 men as part of the Grande Armée's invasion of Russia and fighting on the southern flank it did not suffer the fate of the rest of the army. In February 1813 Austria announced its neutrality, although the army was far from ready to fight. The German infantry regiments had been reduced from three to two battalions with the battalions reduced to only 300 men. Cavalry regiments had also been reduced, from 6 squadrons to 4 for the heavies and from 8 to 6 for the lights. However, even these paper strengths had not been met so the army needed to be expanded rapidly with equipment of all kinds being in short supply. In May 1813 the Kaiser authorised the formation of a 120,000 strong Army of Bohemia and the following month the mobilisation of 50,000 Landwehr. Most of the Landwehr were to be distributed as individual battalions among the regular divisions.

Austrian Grenzer

CUSTOMIZED ARMY

Choose an army based on the maxima and minima in the list below. The following special instructions apply to this army:

- All infantry move as **Unreformed** but fire as **Reformed.** They are paid for as **Unreformed.**
- At least 1 and no more than 2 mixed divisions may be used.
- Jaegers and grenzers, including all skirmisher attachments, must all be in the same mixed division.
- Jaegers may not be used in *Skirmisher* formation.
- *Irregular* grenzers MUST only be used in *Skirmisher* formation.
- Either may be used as skirmisher attachments.
- A single unit of cuirassiers may be used in a mixed division, which may additionally contain infantry, artillery and a single unit of light horse.
- A single unit of Grenadiers may be attached from reserve to an infantry division.
- One medium artillery unit may have a single heavy artillery attachment if no heavy artillery unit is used.
- Attachments must be allocated as follows:
- Attachments must be allocated to units in non-mixed divisions when the army is first created.
- Attachments for mixed divisions must be allocated after terrain placement and immediately before deployment.

AUSTRIAN CORPS 1813

Territory Type:	Southern Europe, Central Europe
Initiative Level:	1

Commanders

Command Level	Quality	Points per General	Minimum	Maximum	
Corps Commander	Exceptional	80	1		
	Skilled	50			
	Competent	30			
Division Commander	Skilled	50	2	2	4
	Competent	30		3	

Unit Name	Troop Type	Elan	Training	Special Capabilities	Points per base	Bases per unit	Minimum bases	Maximum bases	
Core Infantry									
Hungarian Infantry	Line Infantry	Average	Drilled	-	8	4 or 6	6	12	48
German Infantry	Line Infantry	Average	Drilled	-	8	4	12	16	
			Conscript		6	4 or 6	12	24	
6 pdr Field Artillery	Medium Artillery	Average	Drilled	-	20	2 or 3	3	6	7
12 pdr Field Artillery	Heavy Artillery	Average	Drilled	-	24	2	0	2	
Core Cavalry									
Hussars	Light Cavalry	Superior	Drilled	-	11	4 or 6	10	6	16
		Average			8			12	
Chevauxleger	Light Cavalry	Average	Drilled	-	8	4 or 6		12	
Optional Units									
Tyrolean Jaegers	Light Infantry	Average	Drilled	Rifles	13	4	0	4	8
Grenzers	Light Infantry	Poor	Drilled	-	6	4	0	4	
		Average	Irregular		7				
German Grenadiers	Line infantry	Average	Veteran	-	10	4 or 6	0	6	
Landwehr and Volunteers	Line infantry	Poor	Conscripts	-	4	4 or 6	0	6	
Austrian Dragoons	Heavy cavalry	Average	Drilled	-	10	4	0	6	
Cuirassiers	Heavy Cavalry	Average	Drilled	Shock	13	4 or 6	0		
6pdr horse artillery	Horse Artillery	Average	Drilled	-	24	2	0	2	

Attachments

Type	Restrictions	Special Capabilities	Points per base	Minimum bases	Maximum bases
Skirmishers	Only in a mixed division with no light infantry. Maximum of 1 per line Infantry unit (not grenadiers)	Muskets	8	0	1 per line infantry
		Rifles	10		
Officers	No more than 1 per division		12	0	1 per division
Artillery	No more than 1 per division for Infantry and Artillery only.	Medium	10	0	1 per division
		Heavy	12	0	
Cavalry	None allowed				

APPENDIX 2 – HISTORICAL BATTLES

THE BATTLE FOR PLANCENOIT
18 JUNE 1815

This pair of lists replicates the struggle for Plancenoit at Waterloo. It was a fierce encounter which lasted several hours ending with the French being driven from Plancenoit and its environs.

The fighting began late in the afternoon with Marshal Blucher and General von Bulow launching an attack, initially with two brigades of Bulow's (IV) Corps supported by IV Corps's reserve cavalry and artillery. The attack was later reinforced by the 12th brigade of the 3rd corps and the 5th brigade from Pirch's II Corps. Their aim was to seize Plancenoit and break into the rear of the French positions. Facing this attack was Lobau's small 6th Corps supported by two cavalry divisions, and reinforced as the battle progressed by the Young Guard and four Old Guard battalions. It is not an equal point battle and some maxima have been exceeded. Two Prussian brigades have been treated as single division and total forces exceed a single Corps on both sides, with each having elements from different Corps.

PRUSSIAN FORCES

Army Commander FM Prince Blucher	*Exceptional charismatic*
IV Corps Lt General Graf Bulow v Dennewitz	*Skilled Corps Commander*
15th Brigade	
Losthin	*Skilled Division Commander*
1x6 bases Musketeers	*Line Infantry, average, veteran*
1x6 bases Landwehr	*Line Infantry, average, conscript*
1x6 bases Landwehr	*Line Infantry, superior, conscript*
1x2 bases 12pdr field artillery	*Heavy artillery, average, drilled*
1x skirmisher attachment	*Rifle*
1x officer attachment	
16th Brigade	
Hiller	*Competent Division Commander*
1x6 bases Musketeers	*Line Infantry, average, veteran*
1x6 bases Landwehr	*Line Infantry, average, conscript*
1x4 bases Landwehr	*Line Infantry, superior, conscript*
1x3 bases 6 pdr field artillery	*Medium artillery, poor, drilled*
1x Skirmisher attachment	*Musket*
1x Cavalry attachment	
Cavalry Division	
Pruessen	*Skilled Division Commander*
1x4 bases Hussars	*Light cavalry, average, veteran*
1x6 bases Hussars	*Light cavalry, average, drilled,*
1x4 bases Uhlans	*Light cavalry, average, drilled, lances*
1x6 bases Landwehr cavalry	*Light cavalry, average, conscript*
1x2 bases 6pdr horse artillery	*Horse artillery, poor, drilled*
1x Officer attachment	
Reinforcements	
12th Brigade	
von Stülpnagel	*Competent Division Commander*
1x6 bases Musketeers	*Line Infantry, average, veteran*

1x6 bases Landwehr	*Line Infantry, average, conscript*
1x4 bases Landwehr	*Line Infantry, superior, conscript*
1x Skirmisher attachment	*Rifle*
1x Cavalry attachment	
5th Brigade	
Tippelskirch	*Competent Division Commander*
1x6 bases Musketeers	*Line Infantry superior veteran*
1x6 bases Musketeers	*Line Infantry average drilled*
1x6 bases Landwehr	*Line Infantry superior conscript*
1x2 bases 6pdr field artillery	*Medium artillery, average, drilled*
1x Officer attachment	
1x Cavalry attachment	

FRENCH FORCES

VI Corps (part) Gen Mouton Count De Lobau	*Skilled Corps Commander*
Infantry Division (19th)	
Zimmer	*Competent division commander*
1x4 bases line Infantry	*Line infantry, average veteran*
1x4 bases line infantry	*Line infantry, average drilled*
1x4 bases line infantry	*Line infantry, average drilled*
1x artillery attachment	
Infantry Division (20th)	
General Jeanin	*Competent Division Commander*
1x4 bases line infantry	*Line infantry, average drilled*
1x4 bases line infantry	*Line infantry, average drilled*
1x2 bases 6pdr field artillery	*Medium artillery, average drilled*
1x Skirmisher attachment	*Musket*
1x Officer attachment	
Cavalry Divison (5th)	
General Subervie	*Competent Division Commander*
1x4 bases chevauleger-lanciers	*Light cavalry, average, veteran, lances*
1x4 bases chevauleger-lanciers	*Light cavalry, average, drilled, lances*
1x4 bases chasseurs a cheval	*Light cavalry, average, drilled*
1x Artillery attachment	
Cavalry Division (3rd)	
General Domon	*Competent Division Commander*
1x6 bases chasseurs a cheval	*Light cavalry, average, drilled*
1x4 bases chasseurs a cheval	*Light cavalry, average, drilled*
1x Artillery attachment	
Young Guard Division	
Count Dusheme	*Skilled Division Commander*
1x6 bases Tirailleurs	*Light infantry, average, drilled, guard*
1x6 bases Voltigeurs	*Light infantry, average, drilled, guard*
1x4 bases Old Guard	*Line infantry, superior, veteran, guard*
1x Skirmisher attachment	*Musket*
1x Officer attachment	

BATTLE OF SACILE 1809

The Battle of Sacile took place on April 16, 1809, between 40,000 Austrians under the Archduke John, and 36,000 French and Italians under Eugène de Beauharnais, Viceroy of Italy.

In April 1809, Austria declared war on France. Archduke John crossed the border into Italy with his army forcing the French to retreat and regroup behind the Tagliamento River. However, pre-empting the threat posed by the troops of Archduke John, Prince Eugène had already positioned his troops on the border in Friuli and Venetia. In particular, General Grenier's 3rd division was positioned in the town of Sacile. Prince Eugène organised a defence of the town in preparation of a counter-attack.

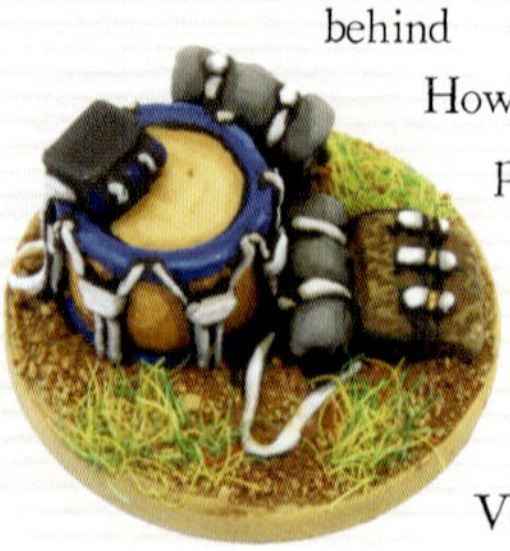

The Austrians arrived at Sacile on 16 April, having been delayed by a string of minor actions at Pordenone and Ospedaletto. The majority of the fighting occurred in the vicinity of the newly constructed bridges over the river. Fighting lasted throughout the morning until an Austrian flank movement, which menaced the French line of retreat, forced Eugène to retire. The French fell back to the Piave River where both sides would meet again.

AUSTRIAN FORCES

Commander in Chief: Archduke John	*Competent Army Commander*
VIII Corps	
Marquis de Chasteler	*Competent Corps Commander*
General of Infantry Albert Gyulai	*Competent Division Commander*
1x6 Line infantry + officer att.	*Line infantry, veteran, drilled*
1x6 Line infantry	*Line infantry, average, drilled*
1x6 Line infantry + officer att.	*Line infantry, average, drilled*
1x6 Line infantry	*Line infantry, average, drilled*
1x6 Line infantry + artillery att.	*Line infantry, average, drilled*
1x4 Line infantry	*Line infantry, average, drilled*
1x2 12pdr field artillery	*Heavy artillery, average, drilled*
1x2 6pdr field artillery	*Medium artillery, average, drilled*
General of Infantry Frimont	*Competent Division Commander*
1x6 Grenzer + Jaeger att.	*Light infantry, average, drilled*
1x6 Cheveux leger + artillery att.	*Light cavalry, average, drilled*
1x6 Hussars	*Light cavalry, superior, drilled*
IX Corps	
Feldmeister Ignaz Gyulai	*Competent Corps Commander*
General of Infantry Volkmann	*Competent Division Commander*
1x6 Grenzers	*Light infantry, average, conscript*
1x4 Hussars	*Light cavalry, superior, drilled*
1x6 Dragoons	*Heavy cavalry, average, veteran*
General of Infantry Besanez	*Skilled Division Commander*
1x6 Line infantry + artillery att.	*Line infantry, average, veteran*
1x6 Line infantry	*Line infantry, average, drilled*
1x6 Line infantry + artillery att.	*Line infantry, average, drilled*
1x6 Line infantry	*Line infantry, average, drilled*
General of Cavalry Reichenberg	*Competent Division Commander*
1x6 Hussars + artillery att.	*Light cavalry, superior, drilled*

1x6 Hussars	*Light cavalry, superior, drilled*
1x6 Grenzers + artillery att.	*Light infantry, average, conscript*
General of Infantry Hager	*Competent Division Commander*
1x4 Grenadiers	*Line infantry, average, veteran*
1x4 Grenadiers	*Line infantry, average, veteran*
1x6 Dragoons + artillery att.	*Heavy cavalry, average, veteran*

FRENCH ARMY OF ITALY

Commander In Chief: Eugene de Beauharnais	*Skilled Army commander*
1st Division	
General Serras	*Skilled Corps Commander*
1x6 French Infantry	*Line infantry, average, veteran*
1x6 French Infantry	*Line infantry, average, drilled*
1x6 French Infantry	*Line infantry, average, drilled*
1x4 Chasseur a Cheval	*Light cavalry, average, drilled*
1x Artillery attachment	
2nd Division	
General Broussier	*Competent Division Commander*
1x6 French Infantry	*Line infantry, average, drilled*
1x6 French Infantry	*Line infantry, average, drilled*
1x6 French Infantry	*Line infantry, average, drilled*
1x2 4pdr/8pdr Field artillery	*Medium artillery, average, drilled*
1x Officer Attachment	
3rd Division	
General Grenier	*Skilled Division Commander*
1x6 French Infantry	*Line infantry, average, veteran*
1x6 French Infantry	*Line infantry, average, drilled*
1x6 French Infantry	*Line infantry, average, drilled*
1x2 4pdr/8pdr Field artillery	*Medium artillery, average, drilled*
4th Division	
General Barbou	*Skilled Division Commander*
1x6 French Infantry	*Light infantry, average, veteran*
1x4 French Infantry	*Line infantry, average, drilled*
1x6 French Infantry	*Line infantry, average, drilled*
1x6 French Infantry	*Line infantry, average, drilled*
1x2 4pdr/8pdr Field artillery	*Medium artillery, average, drilled*
1x Officer Attachment	
1st Italian Division	
General Severoli	*Competent Division Commander*
1x6 Italian Infantry + skirmisher att.	*Line infantry, average, veteran*
1x4 Italian Infantry + artillery att.	*Line infantry, average, drilled*
1x4 Italian Infantry + cavalry att.	*Line infantry, average, drilled*
Light Cavalry Division	
General Sahuc	*Skilled Division Commander*
1x4 French Chasseur a Cheval	*Light cavalry, average, drilled*
1x4 French Chasseur a Cheval	*Light cavalry, average, drilled*
1x4 French Chasseur a Cheval	*Light cavalry, average, drilled*
1x4 French Hussar	*Light cavalry, superior, drilled*
1x Artillery attachment	

ARTWORK REFERENCES

Page 5: *79th Highlanders at Waterloo, by Graham Turner © Osprey Publishing Ltd. Taken from Warrior* 20: British Redcoat 1793–1815.

Page 9: *The Armée du Nord, by Christa Hook © Osprey Publishing Ltd. Taken from Warrior* 57: French Napoleonic Infantryman 1803–15.

Page 12: The first Austrian attack on the village of Marengo, by Christa Hook © Osprey Publishing Ltd. Taken from Campaign 70: Marengo 1800.

Page 13: *General Rapp at Austerlitz, by Patrice Courcelle © Osprey Publishing Ltd. Taken from Men-at-Arms* 444: Napoleon's Mounted Chasseurs of the Imperial Guard.

Page 15: *The battle for Telnitz, by Christa Hook © Osprey Publishing Ltd. Taken from Campaign* 101: Austerlitz 1805.

Page 19: Skirmish in the streets of Casteggio, by Christa Hook © Osprey Publishing Ltd. Taken from Campaign 70: Marengo 1800.

Page 21: General der Kavallerie von Melas and Generalmajor Zach before the battle of Marengo, by Christa Hook © Osprey Publishing Ltd. Taken from Campaign 70: Marengo 1800.

Page 22: 95th Rifles skirmishing, by Christa Hook © Osprey Publishing Ltd. Taken from Warrior 47: British Rifleman 1797–1815.

Page 23: *The storming of Medy-bas, by Steve Noon © Osprey Publishing Ltd. Taken from Warrior* 62: Prussian Regular Infantryman 1808–15

Page 73: *The battle of Somosierra, by Patrice Courcelle © Osprey Publishing Ltd. Taken from Men-at-Arms* 440: Napoleon's Polish Lancers of the Imperial Guard.

Page 75: *The charge of the Russian Imperial Guard, by Christa Hook © Osprey Publishing Ltd. Taken from Campaign* 101: Austerlitz 1805.

Page 81: *Tirailleurs of the Young Guard, by Richard Hook © Osprey Publishing Ltd. Taken from Warrior* 22: Imperial Guardsman 1799–1815

Page 90: 85th Foot at the village of Pozo Bello, by Patrice Courcelle © Osprey Publishing Ltd. Taken from Campaign 99: Fuentes de Oñoro 1811.

Page 91: *The battle of Nazareth, by Christa Hook © Osprey Publishing Ltd. Taken from Warrior* 77: French Soldier in Egypt 1798–1801.

Page 93: *La Haye Sainte, by Christa Hook © Osprey Publishing Ltd. Taken from Warrior* 47: British Rifleman 1797–1815.

Page 100: Portuguese artillery, by Patrice Courcelle © Osprey Publishing Ltd. Taken from Campaign 99: Fuentes de Oñoro 1811.

Page 102: Imperial escort duty, by Richard Hook © Osprey Publishing Ltd. Taken from Warrior 22: Imperial Guardsman 1799–1815.

Page 103: *Clash of lancers, by Patrice Courcelle © Osprey Publishing Ltd. Taken from Men-at-Arms* 433: Napoleon's Scouts of the Imperial Guard.

Page 109: *French revolutionary infantry, by Christa Hook © Osprey Publishing Ltd. Taken from Warrior 63:* French Revolutionary Infantryman 1791–1802.

Page 111: *Grenadiers à cheval at Eylau, by Richard Hook © Osprey Publishing Ltd. Taken from Warrior 22:* Imperial Guardsman 1799–1815

Page 113: *French artillery, by Christa Hook © Osprey Publishing Ltd. Taken from Campaign* 101: Austerlitz 1805.

Page 115: Melee in Fuentes de Oñoro, by Patrice Courcelle © Osprey Publishing Ltd. Taken from Campaign 99: Fuentes de Oñoro 1811.

Page 117: *69th Foot, by Graham Turner © Osprey Publishing Ltd. Taken from Warrior 20:* British Redcoat 1793–1815.

Page 123: *The retreat from Moscow, by Richard Hook © Osprey Publishing Ltd. Taken from Warrior 22:* Imperial Guardsman 1799–1815

Page 135: *Oudinot's advance at Bautzen, by Christa Hook © Osprey Publishing Ltd. Taken from Campaign 87:* Lützen & Bautzen 1813.

INDEX

PLAYSHEETS

The following pages contain playsheets to be used as a Quick Reference Guide while playing the game.

ACTION SEQUENCE

Phase	Action	Description
CP Allocation	CCs allocate command points to DCs	Active player only
Assault	Declare Assaults	Active player only - CMT if required
	Declare responses	Inactive player - CMT or Cohesion Test if required
	Move chargers and adjudicate firing	Active player resolves result and makes Outcome Moves immediately
Firing	Active player fires	Inactive player resolves result and makes Outcome Moves immediately
	Inactive player fires	Active player resolves result and makes Outcome Moves immediately
Movement	Check for reserves and flank marches	Active player only - CMTs if required
	Move units	Active player only - CMTs if required
	Auto-activate reserves	Inactive player only
Combat	Calculate combat hits	Both players simultaneously
	Combat Resolution	Follow steps in 'Combat resolution' table
	Cohesion Tests	Both players - inactive player first
Recovery	Move commanders & restore ADCs	Both players - inactive player first
	Recover cohesion	Active player only - test as required
	Promote commanders	Either Player

THE COHESION TEST (CT)

Command Ranges	Type	Normal	Leading Unit	In Combat	Command Ranges
	Corps	20	10	0	
	Division	8	8	0	
Test type	Attempted activity			Score required	Result if test failed
Responding to an assault	Infantry assaulted by Cavalry in the open & not in Square	Form Square from Extended Line		6+	Cohesion Loss
		Form Square from Tactical or March Column		5+	
		Stand and fire			
	Note: Infantry not in square take an additional automatic cohesion loss if assaulted by cavalry starting from within 2MU				
	Any friendly unit burst through by impetuous troops			5+	Cohesion Loss
	Infantry in Square assaulted by other Infantry				
	A Wavering unit having an assault declared on it				
	Light Cavalry Skirmishers choosing to counter-charge non-Skirmisher cavalry				Evade
	Artillery choosing to stand and fire			4+	Abandon Guns
Recovery tests	Rallying broken unit		1 attempt only	6+	Unit Destroyed
	Recovering abandoned Artillery	3 cohesion losses			
		1 or 2 cohesion losses		5+	
	Recovering cohesion losses for any unit				No effect
Other cohesion tests	Whenever Broken non-Skirmishing Infantry first passes within 4MUs			5+	Cohesion Loss
	If within 4MU of non-Skirmishing cavalry at the time they break				
	If 'burst through' by friends as part of an outcome move				
	When a Commander of any type with the unit becomes a casualty				
Number of dice used for tests	Training level	Veterans	Drilled	Irregulars	Conscripts
	Dice used	3	2	2	1
	Charismatic commander with unit		+1 dice	Does not affect artillery	
	Conscripts		+1 dice	If in defensive position or with rear support	
	Troops in extended line:		-1 dice	If not defending obstacle, or hill/slope	

ABANDONED GUNS

Action forcing abandonment (of unlimbered artillery):			Cohesion losses
Voluntary Retire to Infantry unit within 2MU when charged			-1 cohesion
Otherwise:	If forced to retire by failing a test	Retiring from Infantry assault	
		Retire from cavalry Assault	-2 cohesion
	Retire as an outcome move from combat		
Additional loss if all friends within 2MU retire (once only)			-1 cohesion
* An abandoned artillery unit accumulating more than 3 cohesion level losses is permanently destroyed.			

CASUALTIES TO COMMANDERS:

A player rolls to injure a commander if he causes 3 hits in a single phase on his unit

Commander type	Number of dice to roll	Hits from Shooting		Hits from Combat	
		Rifles	Muskets/Artillery	Enemy retires	any other result
Corps Commander	3	5+	6+	5+	6+
Division Commander	2				
Brigade Commander	1				

All dice rolled must be equal to or above the required number

MOVEMENT TABLE

Unit type		Open	Rough	Difficult
Unreformed Infantry	In tactical or extended line	4	3	2
Reformed Infantry	In extended Line	3	2	1
	In tactical formation	6	4	2
Any Infantry	In march column	6	4	4
	In skirmish formation		6	4
Unlimbered Artillery	move by prolong - if any guns are heavy	2	1	N/A
	move by prolong - with no heavy guns		2	1
Limbered Artillery	Foot Artillery	6	4	2
	Horse artillery	10		
Cavalry	Heavy	8	6	2
	Regular Light uness in single rank	10		4
	In single rank, Irreg light or in March Column		8	6
Corps or Divisional Commander moving on his own				
Units in Column of March & limbered artillery move double distance on a road if they stay outside 6MUs of all enemy units				
Colour Coding	No disordering effect		Unit fires and fights as if 1 Cohesion level lower	
	N/A = Not allowed		Unit fires and fights as if 2 Cohesion levels lower	

THE COMPLEX MOVE TEST (CMT)

Phase	Activity			Steady/Disordered	Wavering
Assault Phase Only	Assault through friends unless Skirmishers, Artillery or own Div.			Complex	N/A
	Infantry assaulting a target also being assaulted by Cavalry				
	Mounted Skirmishers assaulting Steady or Disordered non-Skirm.				
	Assault if Disordered or Spent & not Guard, Shock or Impetuous				
	Any other assault declaration by a unit in command range			Simple	
	Impetuous cavalry ordered not to assault when in assault reach			Complex	
	Attempt to assault when out of command range				
	Counter-charge if Cavalry			Simple	N/A
	Make an intercept move if steady				
	Make an intercept move if Disordered or Spent			Complex	
	Continue into contact after receiving 1 or 2 hits during charge				
Combat phase	Disordered cavalry wishing to 'pass through' enemy infantry			Complex	N/A
Movement Phase Only	Activating an off-table command			Complex	N/A
	Any forwards move including a wheel with no change of formation			Simple	Simple
	Turn or wheel to face enemy within 2MU				
May always make a simple move if test is failed	A change of formation or facing while otherwise stationary		> 2MU from enemy		Complex
			<= 2MU of enemy	Complex	N/A
	Slide 1 base sideways if otherwise stationary and over 2MU from enemy				
	Pass through friends in any direction	Either unit is Skirmishers or Artillery		Simple	Simple
		If both units of same command			Complex
		If units are of different commands		Complex	
	Move including 180deg turn before and/or after	Up to full move in line or march	End facing original rear	Complex	Complex
		1/2 move in any formation	End facing original front or rear		
		Up tp full move if Skirmishers		Simple	Simple
If making a double move, the first move must be completed (and successful) before 2nd move is attempted.	Skirmishers moving 1/2 distance in any direction if outside 2MU			Simple	Simple
	Crossing obstacle or entering buildings forwards or backwards		Skirmishers		
			Non-Skirmishers	Complex	Complex
	Artillery only	Unlimber		Complex	N/A
		Move by prolong forwards or backwards			Complex
		Limber	Heavy Artillery		
			Medium Artillery	Simple	
	2nd move if over 6MU from enemy throughout			Complex	N/A

	Type of move	Score required	Commander leading	In command	Out of command
Score required to pass a CMT	Simple	Auto	Auto	No CP required	
	Complex	5+	4+	1 CP required	2 CPs required
	N/A	Not allowed - Unit cannot perform this action			
Re-rolls	Superior:	Guards:	Superior Guards:	Poor:	Re-rolls
	Re-roll 1's	Re-roll 1's	Re-roll 1's and 2's	Re-roll 6's	
A Complex move requires a CP unless it is the first CMT taken this phase for a unit led by a commander.					
A unit must successfully complete its 1st move before the CMT for a 2nd move is attempted.					
A move may include a slide sideways up to 1 base width if > 6MU from enemy or to avoid friends if closer. A stationary unit requires a CMT.					
A Wavering unit may not move to within 10MU of an anemy unit, or closer to any enemy if already within 10MU.					

FIRING

Number of Dice Used

Close (musket) range:		0 to 2 MU
Unit Type	**Small unit**	**Large Unit**
Infantry in Tactical	4	6
Each 1/2 of Ext Line		
Artillery (not mortars)	6	8
Square or skirmishers	3	4
Artillery attachment *	+2 dice	
Square with art att.	+1 dice	
Supporting unit - inf	+1 dice	
Supporting unit - art	+2 dice	
* Rocket attachments cannot fire at short or medium range		

Medium (skirmishing/canister) Range:		2 to 6 MU
Unit Type	**Small unit**	**Large Unit**
Non-reformed infantry	0	0
Non-reformed + sk att.	3	4
Reformed line infantry		
Reformed + sk att.	4	5
Light infantry	5	6
Artillery (not mortars)	6	8
Artillery attachment (see notes)	+2 dice if firing separately	
	+1 dice otherwise	
Enemy cavalry in 6MU	-1 dice if rifles, -2 dice if muskets	

Long (round shot) Range:		6 to 16 MU
Mortars & Heavy art.	4	5
Medium artillery	3	4
Artillery attachment	+1 dice	

Cohesion Losses:	Disordered	Lose 1 dice per 3
	Wavering	Lose 1 dice per 2
	Broken	no firing
Rain & Snow	Fire at 1 cohesion level lower	

THE TO-HIT SCORE

Target	Range	Score	Points of Advantage (POA)	
In single rank	Long	6+	Target is in March Column or Square, or firers are behind flank or rear, or target is in deep formation at long range	+
Unlimbered Art.				
On soft ground				
Infantry in any formation *	Close	4+	Target is in Skirmisher formation	–
			Skirmishers firing at close range	
Cavalry charging firers *			Target in cover fired at by:	
			Rockets, Howitzers, Mortars, Siege artillery	no POA
All other targets	Any	5+	All other firing at targets in cover	–
			Only artillery can fire at troops 'occupying' buildings	
Re-rolls	Veterans:	Conscripts:	Irregulars:	net + POA = add 1 to dice score
	Re-roll 1's	Re-roll 6's	Re-roll 6's	net – POA = subtract 1 from dice score
A steady or disordered large unit reduces the number of hits by 1 before consulting the Results table.				
A Superior regiment reduces the number of hits by 1 before consulting the Results table - only during a charge				
* If target is charging firers and starting charge partially to firers front.				The To-Hit score cannot be higher than 6+

RESULTS OF FIRING

Number of hits	Result		Cohesion loss
0	No effect on movement		No effect
1	CMT to Advance	Cavalry must retire to 3MU if closer.	
2			-1 cohesion
3	Retire to 3MU if closer or are Wavering, otherwise may not advance.		-1 cohesion
4+	Retire immediately as per Outcome Moves table		-2 cohesion *
* A unit can only drop 1 cohesion level if all fire is at medium or long range.			
* A Wavering unit losing cohesion at medium or long range retires as per Outcome Table instead. (squares change to tactical)			
* A Guard unit can never drop by more than 1 cohesion level from firing in a single phase even at close range.			

OUTCOME MOVES

Unit type	Situation		Cohesion state: Disrupted	Wavering / Evading	Broken
Infantry	If facing cavalry and defending obstacle or in square		Halt	Halt	Destroyed
	In the open and in contact with cavalry		Retire D6	Retire D6 +2	
	Otherwise				Retire D6 +4
Cavalry	In contact with enemy		Retire D6 + 2	Retire D6 +4	Retire D6 +6
	Otherwise				
Limbered artillery	In contact with enemy		Retire D6	Retire D6 +2	Destroyed
	Otherwise				Retire D6 +4
Unlimbered artillery	In contact with enemy cavalry		Abandoned	Destroyed	Destroyed
	In contact with enemy infantry			Abandoned	
	Otherwise:	Foot Artillery	Retire D6	Retire D6 +2	Retire D6 +4
		Horse Artillery	Retire D6 +2	Retire D6 +4	Retire D6 +6
Minimum retire distance is 3MU		Any in skirmish formation and limbered horse artillery retire an additional 2MU			
Distance is halved in difficult terrain		Infantry in square retiring more than 3MU end in Tactical formation			
A unit retiring >= its normal move ends facing the direction moved, otherwise it faces the direction it moved from.					

COMBAT

Dice Allowance		
Unit type	**Small Unit**	**Large Unit**
Infantry or Cavalry in Tactical or Extended Line except Irregular light cavalry	6	8
All other troops or situations	4	6

DICE ADDITIONS AND LOSSES

Lancers vs Infantry and/or Artillery		+2 (+1) dice	* (+1) Units partially lancers or uphill get +1 instead of +2 (Unless lancers are Wavering)	
Enemy downhill		+2 (+1) dice		
Each supporting unit to flank		+2 dice	Unless either side is defending an obstacle	
Unit has rear support		+1/-1 dice	See Rear Support for details	
Shock Cavalry vs Infantry or light Cavalry		+1/-1 dice	Unless Infantry is in Square or defending an obstacle	
Cavalry with artillery attachment		+1 dice	Only against other Cavalry or Infantry in Square	
Cohesion losses:	Disordered	Wavering	Broken	Infantry and artillery in rain or snow fight as 1 cohesion level lower
	Lose 1 dice per 3	Lose 1 dice per 2	None	

THE TO-HIT SCORE

Normal score required	4+	Modified by the POAs below
Points of Advantage (POA)		
Attacking enemy flank or rear	+/–	Attacker has + POA, defender has – POA
Mounted facing lighter Cavalry	+	Against other mounted only
Mounted fighting Artillery	+	Unless Artillery is defending an obstacle or in cover
Mounted fighting Infantry not in Square	+	Unless infantry are defending an obstacle or in cover
Mounted fighting Infantry in Square	–	Unless Infantry are defending an obstacle (see below)
Fighting across an obstacle	–	Both sides
Infantry facing Shock Cavalry	–	Only in open terrain
March column, Skirmishers or Artillery	–	In any terrain

Re-rolls	Superior:	Guards:	Superior Guards:	Poor:	General leading
	Re-roll 1's	Re-roll 1's	Re-roll 1's and 2's	Re-roll -6's	Improve re-roll by 1

EFFECT OF COMBAT HITS

Hits received	0-1	2-3	4-5	6+
Cohesion losses	0	1	2	3
Guard only:	0	1	1	2
* A large unit reduces the number of hits by 1 before consulting this table.				

COMBAT RESOLUTION

Players perform the following steps in order			
Retire Broken Units			
Non-active player	Retires units in contact and Broken	Active player	May pursue * unless Wavering.
Recovery	Active players Broken units no longer in contact	because of enemy retiring	are recovered to Wavering
Active player	Retires units in contact and Broken	Non-active player	May pursue * unless Wavering
Retire Wavering Units			
Non-active player	Retires units in contact and Wavering	Active player	May pursue * unless Wavering
Active player	Retires units in contact and Wavering	Non-active player	May pursue * unless Wavering
Retire Disordered Units			
Non-active player	Retires units in contact and Disordered	Active player	Halt - no pursuit
Active player	Retires units in contact and Disordered	Non-active player	Halt - no pursuit
Special rules:			
Pass through	Steady Cavalry MUST pass through and Disordered Cavalry MAY pass through if still incontact with Infantry		
Cavalry	Cavalry become Spent and must remove a base if receiving a hit from any source - unless already Spent		
* Infantry do not pursue if in square or defending obstacle.		* Artillery never pursue	
* Infantry may choose not to pursue if there are any unbroken enemy Cavalry regiments within 6MU of their starting position			

PURSUIT

Action	Unit/distance	Steady	Disordered
PURSUE	Artillery	Not allowed	
PURSUE	Infantry D6 MU	Cannot pursue if defending obstacle, or in square. May always occupy buildings	
PURSUE	Infantry D6 MU	CMT to not pursue	CMT to pursue
PURSUE	Cavalry D6 +2MU	Must pursue	CMT to not pursue
Pass through	Cavalry D6 +2MU	Move to enemy rear before measuring distance moved. Otherwise retire	
Superior troops MUST re-roll 1's Poor troops MUST re-roll 6's			